# The Pacific Crest Bicycle Trail

Bil Paul

Bittersweet Publishing Company
Livermore, California

Cover design by Mac Smith.

Front cover: Author (right) and riding partner Patrick Wickman at 9,945-foot Tioga Pass, the highest point on the Pacific Crest Bicycle Trail and the eastern entrance to Yosemite National Park.

All other photographs by author.

Library of Congress Catalog Card Number: 90-84004
International Standard Book Number: 0-931255-06-6

Published by Bittersweet Publishing Company
P.O. Box 1211, Livermore, California 94551

Printed in the United States of America on recycled paper.

*To Harry Patrick Paul*

*my brother*

*who loved nature*

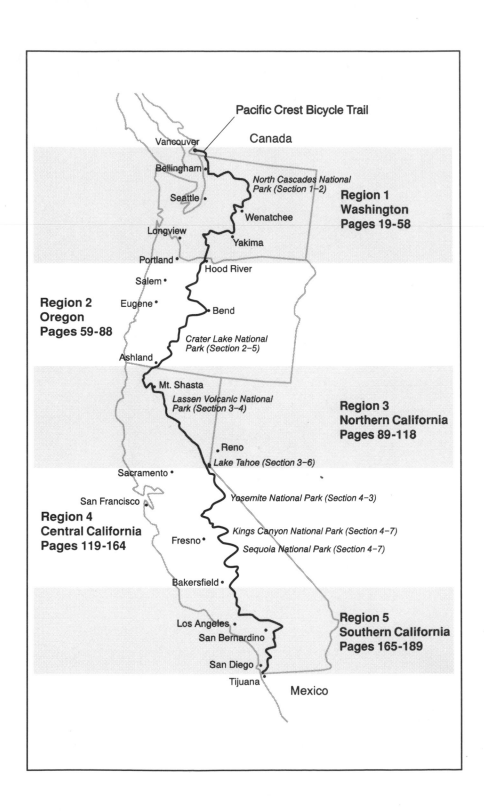

Pacific Crest Bicycle Trail

Canada

Vancouver

Bellingham

North Cascades National
Park (Section 1-2)

Seattle

Wenatchee

**Region 1
Washington
Pages 19-58**

Longview

Yakima

Portland

Hood River

Salem

**Region 2
Oregon
Pages 59-88**

Eugene

Bend

Crater Lake National
Park (Section 2-5)

Ashland

Mt. Shasta

Lassen Volcanic National
Park (Section 3-4)

**Region 3
Northern California
Pages 89-118**

Reno

Lake Tahoe (Section 3-6)

Sacramento

Yosemite National Park (Section 4-3)

San Francisco

**Region 4
Central California
Pages 119-164**

Kings Canyon National Park (Section 4-7)

Fresno

Sequoia National Park (Section 4-7)

Bakersfield

Los Angeles

San Bernardino

**Region 5
Southern California
Pages 165-189**

San Diego

Tijuana

Mexico

# Contents

INTRODUCTION . . . . . . . . . . . . . . . . . . . . . . . . . 8

WEATHER CONDITIONS . . . . . . . . . . . . . . . . . . . . 12

HOW TO USE THIS BOOK . . . . . . . . . . . . . . . . . . 16

REGION 1: WASHINGTON . . . . . . . . . . . . . . . . . . 19

    1-1   Vancouver, BC to Sedro Woolley . . . . . . . . . . . . . . . 20
    1-2   Sedro Woolley to Diablo Lake . . . . . . . . . . . . . . . . 28
    1-3   Diablo Lake to Twisp . . . . . . . . . . . . . . . . . . . . . 32
    1-4   Twisp to Lincoln Rock State Park . . . . . . . . . . . . . . 36
    1-5   Lincoln Rock State Park to Ellensburg . . . . . . . . . . . 40
    1-6   Ellensburg to Rimrock Lake . . . . . . . . . . . . . . . . . 44
    1-7   Rimrock Lake to Council Lake . . . . . . . . . . . . . . . 48
    1-8   Council Lake to Hood River, OR . . . . . . . . . . . . . . 56

REGION 2: OREGON . . . . . . . . . . . . . . . . . . . . . . 59

    2-1   Hood River to Clackamas Lake . . . . . . . . . . . . . . . 60
    2-2   Clackamas Lake to Suttle Lake . . . . . . . . . . . . . . . 64
    2-3   Suttle Lake to Davis Lake . . . . . . . . . . . . . . . . . . 68
    2-4   Davis Lake to Diamond Lake . . . . . . . . . . . . . . . . 74
    2-5   Diamond Lake to Willow Lake . . . . . . . . . . . . . . . 78
    2-6   Willow Lake to Ashland . . . . . . . . . . . . . . . . . . . 84

REGION 3: NORTHERN CALIFORNIA . . . . . . . . . . . . 89

    3-1   Ashland, OR to Hamburg . . . . . . . . . . . . . . . . . . 90
    3-2   Hamburg to Weed . . . . . . . . . . . . . . . . . . . . . . 98
    3-3   Weed to Hat Creek . . . . . . . . . . . . . . . . . . . . . .102
    3-4   Hat Creek to Lake Almanor . . . . . . . . . . . . . . . . .106
    3-5   Lake Almanor to Cottonwood Campground . . . . . . . . .110
    3-6   Cottonwood Campground to South Lake Tahoe . . . . . . .114

REGION 4: CENTRAL CALIFORNIA . . . . . . . . . . . . . .119

    4-1   South Lake Tahoe to Chris Flat Campground . . . . . . . .120
    4-2   Chris Flat Campground to Tuolumne Meadows . . . . . . .124
    4-3   Tuolumne Meadows to Yosemite Valley . . . . . . . . . . .128
    4-4   Yosemite Valley to Bass Lake . . . . . . . . . . . . . . . .132
    4-5   Bass Lake to Shaver Lake . . . . . . . . . . . . . . . . . .136

REGION 4: CENTRAL CALIFORNIA (continued)

    4-6  Shaver Lake to Camp 4$^1$/$_2$ . . . . . . . . . . . . . . . . . . . 140
·  4-7  Camp 4$^1$/$_2$ to Three Rivers . . . . . . . . . . . . . . . . . . 146
    4-8  Three Rivers to Camp Nelson . . . . . . . . . . . . . . . . 152
    4-9  Camp Nelson to Wofford Heights . . . . . . . . . . . . 156
    4-10 Wofford Heights to Tehachapi . . . . . . . . . . . . . . . 160

REGION 5: SOUTHERN CALIFORNIA . . . . . . . . . . . . . . . . . 165

    5-1  Tehachapi to Monte Cristo Campground . . . . . . . . . . 166
    5-2  Monte Cristo Campground to Big Pines Ranger Station . . . . 170
    5-3  Big Pines Ranger Station to Big Bear Lake . . . . . . . . . . 174
    5-4  Big Bear Lake to Idyllwild . . . . . . . . . . . . . . . . . . 178
    5-5  Idyllwild to Julian . . . . . . . . . . . . . . . . . . . . . 182
    5-6  Julian to Mexican Border . . . . . . . . . . . . . . . . . . 186

WHAT TO TAKE . . . . . . . . . . . . . . . . . . . . . . . . . 191

TOURING SAFETY . . . . . . . . . . . . . . . . . . . . . . . . 196

INFORMATION AND RESERVATIONS . . . . . . . . . . . . . . . . 197

OTHER RESOURCES . . . . . . . . . . . . . . . . . . . . . . . 199

ABOUT THE AUTHOR . . . . . . . . . . . . . . . . . . . . . . . 200

Riding the Sisters shortcut in Oregon.

# Introduction

This book describes a mountainous, road-based, bicycling version of the famous Pacific Crest (Hiking) Trail, a challenging Canada-to-Mexico trail along the crest of the Cascade, Sierra Nevada, and Southern California mountains. Completing that trail in one season has been a badge of honor among backpackers. Likewise, completing the Pacific Crest Bicycle Trail in one trip would be a similar milestone for cyclists, especially if carrying camping and cooking gear.

The hiking trail takes virtually an entire summer to complete; this bicycle trail can be completed in a little over a month. Of course, most cyclists will choose to bicycle portions of the trail.

The Pacific Crest Bicycle Trail attempts to come as close as possible to the Pacific Crest (Hiking) Trail while almost entirely using paved roads. A paved road alternate route is usually offered where the main route uses non-paved roads. Alternate routes to scenic Mount St. Helens and Kings Canyon are also offered.

In certain areas, adequate roads do not exist near the Pacific Crest (Hiking) Trail and the bicycle route must descend to lower elevations. Still, the two trails intersect each other no less than 27 times.

This book preserves the backpacking-camping emphasis of the hiking trail by listing in the text and showing on the maps all campgrounds close to the route that permit tent camping. At the end of the book you will find hints on what to take.

On the other hand, for those who would rather travel light and fast, there are plenty of restaurants and motel accommodations along this route if your travel is planned properly. Food stores abound along most of the route, although a reserve should always be carried.

The main route is 2,500 miles long, and the book is divided into five regions, which roughly cover state border and geographical transitions. The five regions include:

### Region 1 — Washington

- Southern British Columbia
- The Cascade Range
- The Columbia River flatlands
- Mount St. Helens and Mt. Adams uplands

### Region 2 — Oregon

• The Cascade Range
• Mt. Hood
• Upland lakes
• Crater Lake National Park

### Region 3 — Northern California

• Mt. Shasta
• Lassen Volcanic National Park
• The transition between the Cascades and the Sierra Nevada
• Lake Tahoe

### Region 4 — Central California

• The Sierra Nevada
• Yosemite National Park
• Kings Canyon National Park
• Sequoia National Park

### Region 5 — Southern California

• High desert country
• The mountains surrounding the Los Angeles basin
• The semi-arid hills and mountains of the San Diego area

The regions are divided into 36 sections ranging from 42 to 97 miles. The average is 70 miles. These sections approximate my days of travel and are used for ease of book layout only — you will certainly travel different daily distances. Travel is described in a north-to-south direction because prevailing winds are generally from the northwest. If one is riding from south to north, the maps and elevation profiles should erase any difficulties found in following the "turn-rights" and "turn-lefts" in the text.

While reading the book, keep in mind that descriptions of weather, temperatures, and traffic are in terms of typical summer conditions (June-July-August).

This book is an outgrowth of an earlier book, now out of print, titled *Bicycling California's Spine: Touring the Length of the Sierra Nevada.* Published in 1981, it covered an area from Mt. Lassen in Northern California to Lake Isabella at the southern end of the Sierra Nevada. Its success spurred me to a nine-year project which culminated in this expanded, border-to-border mountain route.

The comment inevitably arises when talking about a mountainous route: "I'll bet you have to be in good shape." The answer is "yes" if you intend to travel a fair number of miles per day and climb effectively. To prepare for a mountainous bicycle tour, I recommend cycling the hills or mountains in your area carrying the same amount of weight you plan to carry on your trip. If there are no hills in your area, then get a lot of miles on your odometer.

If you will be camping out, try to get some bicycle camping and cooking experience under your belt before attempting a long tour. Make sure you know and trust your gear. Get a good idea of what you really need to take — leave your frying pan at home unless you are going to use it frequently!

Use a sturdy touring or mountain bike with very low gearing. Be experienced in repairs and maintenance, or travel with someone who is. You should be comfortable with your bike. Never, for example, try a new seat on a long tour.

**This book does not guarantee safe passage on the routes it describes.** Certain roads on this route admittedly have hazards and were used only because they are the only ones through a given area. Wear a helmet and do not ride at night. Please refer to the safety section at the rear of the book for more tips. In thousands of miles of touring, I have never had an accident with another vehicle, but I have known people who have. In the final analysis, you are responsible for your own safe trip.

Be aware that campgrounds near Lake Tahoe and in and near national parks are generally full during the summer months. However, there is a campground near Lake Tahoe and a campground in Yosemite Valley reserved solely for cyclists and hikers.

Bicycle touring is habit-forming. I recommend it to anyone who wants to forget the rat race and roam free, breathe fresh air, see the little towns of America, and realize that people are usually generous and friendly.

Touring takes us out of ourselves with the pains and pleasures of physical exertion. We learn to coexist with the elements. We get to know our riding partners even better than we want to. Last but not least, we get to eat prodigiously, deserving every calorie.

I want to take this opportunity to thank my wife Lorraine and my children, Ian, Katie, and Bruce, for giving me the time to ride, write, and draw maps. And thanks to Patrick Wickman, my riding partner for many portions of the trail. Also, the Bellwether Company of San Francisco kindly provided touring equipment and clothing for me to test over the years. Finally, my publisher, Marcus Libkind, has been a joy to work with.

Please write if you discover any changes in the road conditions, stores, or campgrounds described in this book; or if you have any suggestions for improvements. I also would enjoy hearing from anyone who rides the entire route in one trip.

And last of all, I am happy to present my movies of the Pacific Crest Bicycle Trail to bicycle clubs in Central and Southern California.

Bil Paul
P.O. Box 5183
San Jose, CA 95150-5183

A New Zealand couple near Carson Pass in California.

# Weather Conditions

*"A cold front, pushed by strong, gusting winds, dropped six inches of snow on parts of Lassen Volcanic National Park, briefly closing Highway 89. . . Snow is forecast in the Tahoe Valley area, where overnight lows will fall below freezing. . . ."*

San Francisco Chronicle, July 18, 1987

The above quote brings home the fact that mountain weather — like weather everywhere — is full of surprises. However, in the mountains the weather is more extreme than at lower elevations.

One of the nice things about the Pacific Crest Bicycle Trail is that it spends as much time as possible in higher elevations, which are cooler than the flatlands below. However, heat can be a problem during the summer months in the low inland areas of Washington, Oregon, and California.

The following is a breakdown of the weather conditions you may expect along the Trail.

## Winds

This route is described in a north-to-south direction, expecting that cyclists will want to take advantage of predominant winds from the northwest. If there is a storm coming in, the winds may switch to the southwest, but summer storm systems are rare. Count on northwest winds as being the most regular, especially during the summer. However, in mountain areas the local winds can be fickle as they follow valleys and canyons.

## The Further North, The Cooler

According to the dictum that for every 300 miles further north one goes, the temperature should decrease 2 to 3 degrees, then the approximately 1,200 air miles between the Mexican and Canadian borders should produce a temperature differential of 8 to 12 degrees on the average for the same elevation. Likewise, the formula predicts that for every 1,000 feet of additional elevation, the temperature should fall 2 to 3 degrees. This means that you should expect a temperature differential of 6 to 9 degrees between the town of Lee Vining at almost 7,000 feet and Tioga Pass at almost 10,000 feet, although they are located only 11 miles apart.

Putting the north-south and elevation effects together, the temperature at the Mexican border near sea level (inland from the ocean) should be about 18 to 27 degrees warmer on the average than at Rainy Pass at about 5,000 feet on the North Cascades Highway in northern Washington.

Weather Extremes

During portions of the year, parts of this trail are impassable due to snow. For example, the North Cascades Highway in Washington and Tioga Pass in California are both closed in winter, resting peacefully under deep snow-packs. Other portions of the trail may be made more difficult by heat during the summer, especially those low-elevation portions east of the Cascade Mountains in Washington and the low-elevation areas of Southern California.

The discerning touring cyclist will plan his or her trip with these weather extremes in mind. In the following summaries I offer average weather information for the period May 1 to November 1. But be aware that this is average information. As the newspaper quote indicated, in the higher mountain areas snow can appear any time during the summer. Be prepared for the possibility of a rapid turnaround in the weather.

Regions 1 and 2 — Washington and Oregon

Regions 1 and 2, Washington and Oregon, are known for having more precipitation than the rest of the West Coast. Storms which come in from the ocean anywhere over the West Coast during the usual wet season of September through May usually get shunted north during the summer period of May through September, and some of them drop rain on these two northern states.

Looking at sea-level cities like Seattle on the west side of the Cascade Mountains in Oregon and Washington, the average daily high (daytime) temperature in May is about 67 degrees and the average daily low (nighttime) temperature is 46. During the hottest month, July, the average high/low is 79/54. In October the average high/low recedes to 64/45. These are only average temperatures — as you know, temperature records are broken every year.

In the same regions, areas east of the Cascades are not so temperate. A representative city is Yakima at 1,100 feet, close to the Pacific Crest Bicycle Trail, and not far from the Washington-Oregon border. The Yakima average high/low temperatures are 74/43 in May, 89/53 in July, and 66/35 in October.

But in the mountains you can expect cooler temperatures. At 4,000 feet in the central Cascades of Washington, the elevation of some parts of the trail, the average high/low temperatures are 50/35 in May, 64/46 in July, and 47/36 in October.

In Oregon, at 3,800 feet in the Cascades not far from Ashland, the average high/low temperatures are 59/39 in May, 75/51 in July, and 58/42 in October.

Remember, 20-degree variations from these norms are not uncommon and changes can occur rapidly.

You might wonder what your chances are for being rained or snowed on in Washington and Oregon. At 4,000 feet in central Washington, snowfall eases but can still occur in May. In June, snowfall is rare, but unmelted winter snow can remain in shady areas in high elevations into the summer. New snowfalls can begin in October, but are more common in November. Rain at this altitude usually begins easing in May, is least in July, and usually begins picking up again in October.

At 3,800 feet near Ashland, Oregon, May through October can usually be counted on to be snow-free. Rain is minimal from April through September (July and August are the driest months), but rain usually begins in earnest around October.

## Regions 3 and 4 — Northern and Central California

For a sampling of Sierra Nevada weather, data from a 5,000-foot site not far from Lake Tahoe follows. It is contrasted with weather data from the valley city of Fresno at an elevation 300 feet and about 170 air miles south of Lake Tahoe. Keep in mind that the southern end of the Sierra Nevada is ordinarily warmer than the northern end, and that higher elevations will normally be cooler.

At the 5,000-foot site near Lake Tahoe, snow usually begins in October and ends in May. Rain is minimal from May through September and usually picks up in October.

Temperatures at 5,000 feet vary from an average high/low of 60/42 in May, to 77/58 in July, and to 62/45 in October. At the 300-foot level in Fresno the average high/low temperatures are 79/50 in May, 100/65 in July (ouch!!), and 63/38 in October.

When planning to ride at low elevations on high temperature days, get started as early as possible and carry plenty of water.

## Region 5 — Southern California

Generally, the high desert between Tehachapi and Palmdale sees average high/low temperatures of 75/46 in May, 92/61 in July, and 75/43 in October. Precipitation is almost non-existent from May through October.

At Idyllwild, almost directly east of Los Angeles and at an elevation of 5,400 feet, the average high/low temperatures are 68/36 in May, 85/51 in July, and 70/37 in October. Precipitation is rare from May through October.

A low elevation indicator is the city of San Bernardino, between Big Bear Lake and Idyllwild, at an elevation of 1,100 feet. The average high/low temperatures are 80/51 in May, 98/61 in July, and 84/51 in October. Precipitation is also rare during the period from May through October.

At the extreme southern end of the Trail, ocean breezes moderate the weather. In Chula Vista, near the ocean, the average high/low temperatures are 65/55 in May, 71/62 in July, and 71/56 in October. Precipitation is again rare during the period from May through October.

## In Conclusion

Weather exceptions and extremes are common along the Pacific Crest Bicycle Trail. Do not send those warm clothes home prematurely!

*Note that the temperatures in this book are given in degrees Fahrenheit.*

Clouds forming above high mountain ranges can result in brief summer showers. Pictured are the Siskiyou Mountains at the California-Oregon border.

# How To Use This Book

## Maps

The maps in this book are not always oriented with north toward the top of the page — look for the north-pointing arrow on each map to determine the orientation of true north. However, each map overlaps the previous one, which will make connecting one map to the next easy.

The text and maps give mileages rounded off to the nearest whole mile except where they are less than one mile. These mileages were obtained from a variety of sources, including odometer readings, published maps, and books. With this in mind, and because bicycle odometers vary in their accuracy, mileages in this book may not exactly match those given by your odometer.

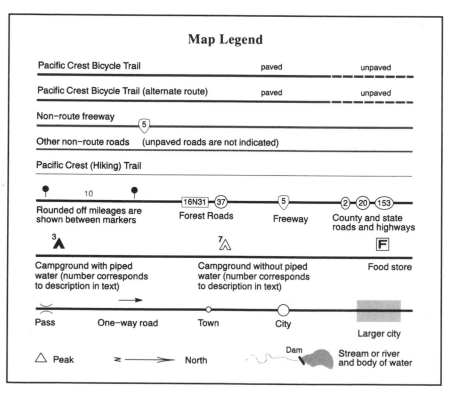

**Map Legend**

Pacific Crest Bicycle Trail                    paved                    unpaved

Pacific Crest Bicycle Trail (alternate route)    paved                    unpaved

Non–route freeway

Other non–route roads    (unpaved roads are not indicated)

Pacific Crest (Hiking) Trail

Rounded off mileages are shown between markers

16N31 – 37    Forest Roads

5    Freeway

2 – 20 – 153    County and state roads and highways

Campground with piped water (number corresponds to description in text)

Campground without piped water (number corresponds to description in text)

F    Food store

Pass          One–way road          Town          City

Larger city

△ Peak          ≈ ——→ North          Dam    Stream or river and body of water

## Elevation Profiles

A book covering mountain touring would not be complete without extensive elevation profiles. In this book they not only offer a concise depiction of climbs and downhills, but also a quick grasp of mileages between locations.

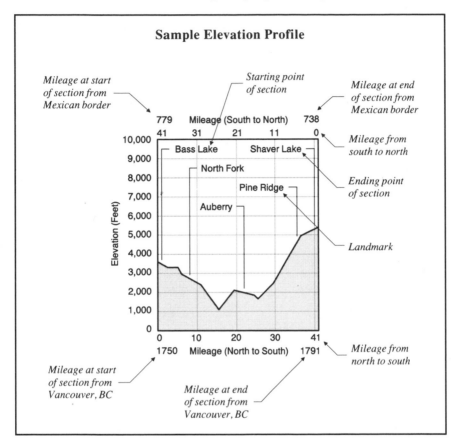

## Campgrounds

Campgrounds which are on or near the Pacific Crest Bicycle Trail and its alternate routes are covered in detail. Each campground shown on a map is accompanied by a number. The number corresponds to a detailed description of the campground in the text. Campground descriptions include location, the availability of water and other facilities, when the campground is open, and who runs it.

When showers and/or flush toilets are mentioned, or if the campground is a state park, it is assumed that drinking water is available. Be aware that the open and closing dates for the campgrounds are approximate and change depending on weather, use, and budgets. Not all campgrounds were personally visited in preparing this book; published information from the Forest Service and other sources was relied upon. If you are traveling early or late in the season you are advised to check in advance.

The price for use of Forest Service, state and municipal campgrounds can vary from nothing to $10 per night. At privately-run campgrounds such as those in the KOA system, prices can exceed $10. What you often get for your money in a private campground is a shower and laundry facilities, a swimming pool, and a store. In a few cases complete campground information was not available.

An impromptu campground is a non-official camping spot without any amenities — no bathrooms, piped drinking water, or prepared campsites.

Finally, be aware that the campground symbols shown on the maps may not be located on the correct side of the road.

## Food and Lodging

This guide assumes that all larger cities have food stores and motels. For rural and small-town areas, an effort is made to indicate food stores in the text and on maps. Motels are not generally covered.

## A Word of Caution

Keep in mind that over time things change. Stores and campgrounds close, and new ones open. Roads are closed or made difficult due to road work; detours are sometimes encountered. Be ready to adapt to these inevitable situations.

# Region 1
# Washington

Early Winter Spires near Washington Pass.

# Vancouver, BC
# to
# Sedro Woolley

*The main route begins at the downtown Vancouver train station and
an alternate route begins at the Vancouver airport.*

## 94 miles • Canadian Accents and Berry Fields

This first section of the Pacific Crest Bicycle Trail, also referred to as "the
Trail," begins in downtown Vancouver, British Columbia and continues
through suburbs before entering primarily rural areas for the remainder of the
trip to Sedro Woolley, Washington. No elevation profile is presented because
this section is relatively flat.

### Main route from the downtown Vancouver train station

Begin this epic route at the Vancouver train station, the arrival and
departure point for Via Rail. Unfortunately, the American AMTRAK only
extends as far north as Seattle, but bus and air connections are available from
Seattle to Vancouver.

From the Vancouver train station, head south on Main Street. After 0.5
mile, bear to the left and enter Kingsway (a business-lined street also known
as Highway 1A/99A). After 5 miles on Kingsway, leave Kingsway and bear
left onto Grange Street just after passing Central Park. Continue as Grange
becomes Dover Street and Dover becomes Oakland Street in a residential
area.

Two miles from the intersection of Kingsway and Grange Street, and at
the top of a hill, turn right onto Walker Avenue at the point where Walker and
Sperling Avenue both intersect with Oakland Street. After 0.7 mile on Walker
Avenue, turn left onto Elwell Street and bike 0.2 mile (passing Richmond
Park) to a right turn onto Mary Avenue. After several blocks, turn left onto
Edmonds Street and bike 0.4 mile to a right turn onto 6 Street. Follow 6 Street
for 0.7 mile to its intersection with 8 Avenue.

*The alternate route from the Vancouver airport joins the main route
from the train station at the corner of 6 Street and 8 Avenue. To
continue on the main route, skip to the section titled "Continuing on
the main route."*

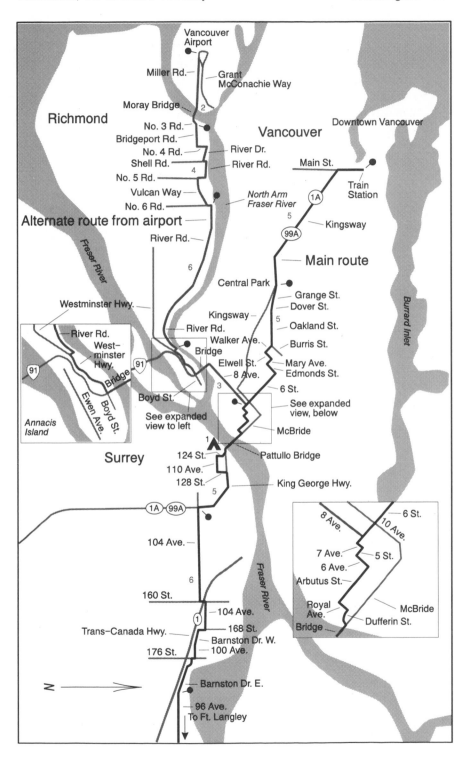

### Alternate route from the Vancouver airport

From the airport follow Miller Road east (it parallels and is just south of Grant McConachie Way) for 2 miles until you cross the Moray Bridge over Moray Channel. Shortly after the bridge, turn left onto Number 3 Road and after one short block turn right onto Bridgeport Road. Follow Bridgeport for 0.7 mile, passing under Highway 99, before making a left turn onto Number 4 Road and traveling 0.3 mile to a right turn onto River Drive. Riding along the North Arm of the Fraser River, follow River Drive for 0.3 mile to a left turn onto Shell Road. After a few feet, turn right onto River Road and travel another 0.3 mile before making a right turn onto Number 5 Road. Ride one block, then turn left onto Vulcan Way and travel another mile through an area of small businesses before making a left turn onto Number 6 Road. Then proceed a short distance to a right turn onto River Road again.

While watching for speeding drivers, bike 6 miles on River Road through a rural area with cranberry bogs and marine industries. Log rafts and towboats are often seen.

At the end of River Road (a short distance after a hard right turn), turn left onto Westminster Highway in the suburb of Queensborough. Proceed 0.8 mile on Westminster Highway as it runs alongside Freeway 91, becomes Boyd Street, and reaches Queensborough Bridge. Do not go under the bridge. Instead, turn right and take a marked bike trail up onto the bridge. The bike route uses the left side of the bridge.

On the other end of the bridge, proceed uphill a short distance on 22 Street (not shown on map) through some concrete car barriers before turning right onto 8 Avenue. Bike 2 miles to 6 Street.

*At the intersection of 6 Street and 8 Avenue the alternate route from the airport joins the main route from the downtown Vancouver train station. Now the combined routes head toward the United States Border.*

### Continuing on the main route

From the intersection of 6 Street and 8 Avenue, follow 6 Street southeast for 2 blocks, turn left onto 7 Avenue, and after one block turn right onto 5 Street. After one more block, turn left onto 6 Avenue. Bike 0.3 mile on 6 Avenue to a right turn onto Arbutus Street. After 0.5 mile on Arbutus, turn left onto Royal Avenue and bike a block or two before turning right onto Dufferin Street. Travel downhill a short distance to the Pattullo Bridge which crosses the Fraser River. Walk your bike on the sidewalk and carefully across a one-way street before making your way to the walkway/bikeway on the right side of the bridge. Bike across the bridge. Just below the far end of the bridge is Fraser River RV Park (#1) with camping. (Note: A number in

A towboat pulls a raft of logs along the North Arm of the Fraser River near Vancouver.

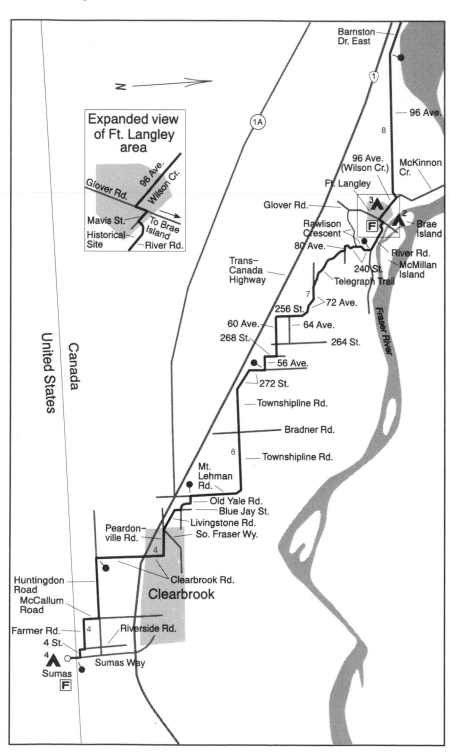

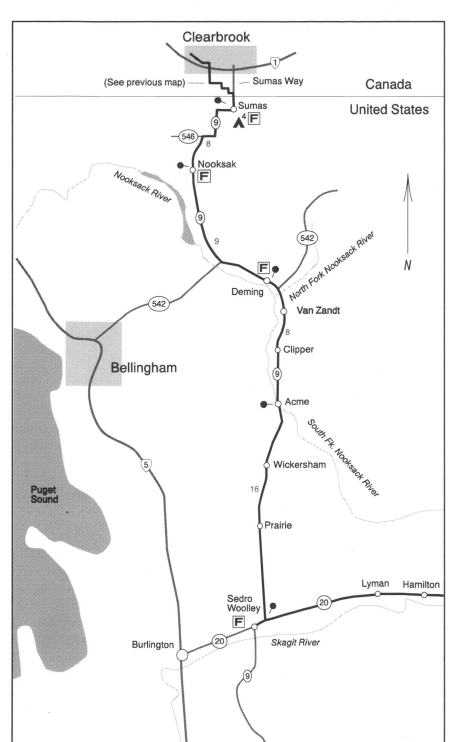

Clearbrook

(See previous map) —          — Sumas Way          Canada

United States

Sumas

546

8

Nooksak

Nooksack River

9

9

542

North Fork Nooksack River

F
Deming

Van Zandt

8

Clipper

9

Bellingham

542

Acme

South Fk. Nooksack River

5

Wickersham

16

Puget
Sound

Prairie

Lyman   Hamilton

Sedro
Woolley

20

Burlington          20          Skagit River

9

N

parentheses after the name of a campground corresponds to its numbered location on the map and to its numbered description at the end of the section.)

After crossing the bridge, follow the walkway as it departs from what is now King George Highway (Highway 1A/99A) and take 124 Street to the right and to the south. After a short distance, turn left onto 110 Avenue and bike 0.3 mile to a left turn onto 128 Street. Shortly thereafter, turn right onto King George Highway. Follow the busy, commercial street for 2 miles before making a left turn onto 104 Avenue and heading east.

After 3 miles on 104 Avenue turn left onto 160 Street. Immediately after crossing Highway 1 (the Trans-Canada Highway), turn right and continue on 104 Avenue, entering a more rural area. One mile after the highway overpass, turn right onto 168 Street and ride south 0.2 mile before turning left onto Barnston Drive West. Barnston becomes 100 Avenue. Turn right onto 176 Street, and shortly afterwards turn left onto Barnston Drive East and ride 1 mile before it becomes 96 Avenue.

Travel east for about 5 miles on 96 Avenue through open country before making a right turn, continuing on 96 Avenue, which takes you into the pleasant, historic city of Ft. Langley. There are several campgrounds here. In Ft. Langley, turn left onto Glover Road and ride a short distance to a right turn onto Mavis Street. After several blocks, turn left onto River Road, which passes the Ft. Langley Historical Site. Fort Langley was the first English settlement in British Columbia.

Ride about 1 mile on River Road before turning right onto 240 Street, which bears right in a wooded area and becomes Rawlison Crescent. After about 0.3 mile, turn left onto 240 Street as that street begins again. Bike 0.5 mile, turn left onto 80 Avenue, and a short distance later turn right and follow Telegraph Trail (a narrow, meandering former stage route) for 1 mile to 72 Avenue.

Turn left onto 72 Avenue and bike about 1 mile to a right turn onto 256 Street. Follow it about 1 mile, approaching Highway 1, before making a left turn onto 60 Avenue. Travel 1 mile on 60 Avenue, turn right onto 268 Street, and go a short distance before turning left onto 56 Avenue. After a short distance on 56 Avenue, turn right onto 272 Street, then bike about 0.6 mile, following the road to where it bends left and parallels Highway 1. After 0.4 mile more, the road bends left again and becomes Townshipline Road.

Follow Townshipline Road for 4 miles, then make a right turn onto Mt. Lehman Road and bike slightly uphill for 2 miles before making a left turn onto Old Yale Road (just before the Highway 1 overpass). After 0.8 mile on Old Yale Road, turn right onto Blue Jay Street which bends to the left and becomes Livingstone Road. Follow Livingstone for 0.8 mile to a left turn onto Peardonville Road (be careful not to get sidetracked on South Fraser Way in the town of Clearbrook). After 0.8 mile on Peardonville, turn right onto Clearbrook Road and cross over Highway 1.

Two miles beyond the overpass, make a left turn onto Huntingdon Road and bike 2 miles before turning right onto McCallum Road. Travel a short distance before taking a left turn onto Farmer Road (the road sign may be missing, but it is the last left turn you can make before McCallum ends at the United States border). Follow Farmer Road a short way before turning right onto Riverside Road. Bike a short distance, turn left onto 4 Street, and shortly thereafter make a right turn onto Sumas Way. A few yards away is the border station.

Crossing the international border at Sumas should be no problem — just get in line with the cars. You will be a welcome change of pace for the Canadian officers.

There is a large grocery store in the town of Sumas, many berry farms populate the area, and ten-thousand-foot-high Mt. Baker looms to the east.

From Sumas, follow Highway 9 forty-one miles to Sedro Woolley. Highway 9 has little traffic and varies from narrow to wide. There are a number of small towns along the way with food stores. The lay of the land is flat until you reach the town of Acme where some gentle hills ensue.

Unfortunately, there are no campgrounds in the vicinity of Sedro Woolley, although there is at least one motel near the city.

## Campgrounds

1. **Fraser River RV Park.** Near the southeast end of the Pattullo Bridge at 11940 Old Yale Road in Surrey. Has restaurant, showers, small grocery store. Open all year. Privately run.

2. **Fort Langley Camping.** From the town of Ft. Langley follow Glover Road north across the Fraser River Bridge onto Brae Island. The campground will be to the left. Has store, laundry, swimming. Open all year. Privately run.

3. **Lombardy Campground.** In the town of Ft. Langley at 9215 McBride Street. Has 5 tent sites, nearby store, indoor pool, hot tub, laundromat. Open all year. Privately run.

4. **Sumas RV Park and Campground.** At the south end of Sumas in Washington (9600 Easterbrook Street) near the U.S.-Canadian border. Has showers, laundromat. Open all year. Privately run.

# Sedro Woolley
# to
# Diablo Lake

63 miles • Following the Skagit River

This gentle section begins in the flatlands around Sedro Woolley, gradually ascends through several towns into a long river valley, and ends at a large, beautiful lake ringed by mountains.

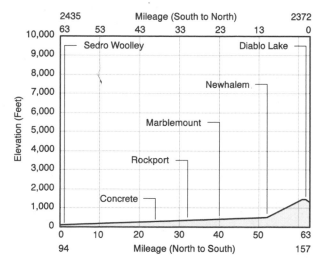

Bicycle east from Sedro Woolley on Highway 20 and follow the sometimes green waters of the Skagit River. Expect to lose the wide shoulder on the road after 13 miles. Twenty-three miles from Sedro Woolley is the town of Concrete. Concrete has a Puget Power Plant Visitors Center at 102 East Main Street that exhibits replicas of nearby dams. Eight miles beyond Concrete is Rockport, and after another 8 miles is the small town of Marblemount.

Several miles past Marblemount you will enter North Cascades National Park. The mountainous terrain of the park was created by glaciation — more than 300 glaciers in the park are still active. The North Cascades Highway (Highway 20), dedicated in 1972, crosses the park along an old rail and truck route originally intended for building and servicing power projects.

After Newhalem there are two short tunnels. In this area you will have to do some climbing, followed by a descent to Diablo Lake and Colonial Creek Campground (#9). The nearest campground to the east is Lone Fir, 39 miles away.

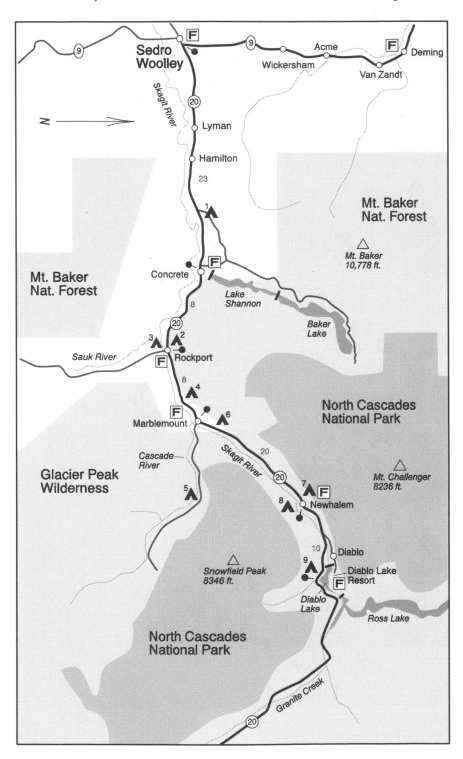

9
Sedro Woolley
F
9
Acme
Wickersham
Van Zandt
F
Deming

N →

Skagit River
20
Lyman
Hamilton
23

Mt. Baker
Nat. Forest

1
F
Concrete
Mt. Baker
10,778 ft.

Mt. Baker
Nat. Forest

Lake
Shannon

Baker
Lake

8
20
3  2
Sauk River
F  Rockport

8
4
F
Marblemount
6

North Cascades
National Park

Cascade
River

Glacier Peak
Wilderness

5

Skagit River
20
20
7  F
Mt. Challenger
8236 ft.
8
Newhalem

10
Diablo
9
Diablo Lake
Resort
F

Snowfield Peak
8346 ft.

Diablo
Lake

Ross Lake

North Cascades
National Park

Granite Creek
20

Wide shoulders along this portion of Highway 20 near the Skagit River make touring a pleasure.

Your last chances for groceries will be at Newhalem and at Diablo Lake Resort (the latter about a mile off Highway 20 near the Diablo Lake Dam).

## Campgrounds

1. **Grandy Creek KOA.** 6 miles west of Concrete on Highway 20, then 0.5 mile north on Russell Road. Has pool. Open 4/1–10/31. Privately run.

2. **Rockport State Park.** 1 mile west of Rockport on Highway 20. Has showers. Open 4/1–11/15. State park.

3. **Howard Miller Steelhead Park.** 1 mile west of Rockport on Highway 20 and across highway from Rockport State Park. Has drinking water. Open all year. County park.

4. **Clark's Skagit River Cabins and RV Park.** 6 miles east of Rockport on Highway 20. Has laundry, restaurant. Open all year. Privately run.

5. **Marble Creek Campground.** 8 miles east of Marblemount on County Road 3528, then 1 mile south on Forest Road 1530. Has drinking water. Open 5/20–9/20. Forest Service.

6. **Alpine Campground.** 2 miles northeast of Marblemount on Highway 20. Has showers, laundromat. Open all year. Privately run.

7. **Goodell Creek Campground.** 1 mile west of Newhalem on Highway 20. Has drinking water. Open all year. Forest Service.

8. **Newhalem Creek Campground.** 1 mile west of Newhalem off Highway 20 and across river from campground #7. Has flush toilets. Open 6/15–9/1. National Park Service.

9. **Colonial Creek Campground.** 10 miles east of Newhalem on Highway 20 near Diablo Lake. Has flush toilets. Open 4/15–11/1. Forest Service.

# Diablo Lake
# to
# Twisp

71 miles • Spectacular Mountains

After a 4,000-foot climb through magnificent scenery to Rainy and Washington Passes — the first long pull of the Trail — the route descends quickly into the Methow River Valley. Then it follows the Methow River gently downhill through warm and usually dry countryside to the cities of Winthrop and Twisp with their many campgrounds.

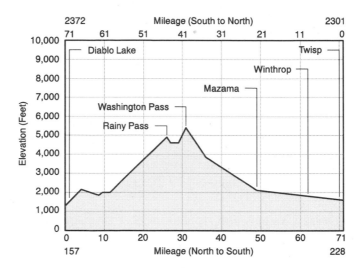

When starting out on this day's ride, keep in mind that the first food store is 49 miles away in Mazama. From Diablo Lake, climb up to several vista points on Highway 20 overlooking Diablo and Ross lakes. After the vista points, there is a minor downhill before the steady, 15-mile climb to 4,860-foot Rainy Pass.

The mountains are beautiful — the most spectacular on the Pacific Crest Bicycle Trail in Washington and Oregon. The first intersection with the Pacific Crest (Hiking) Trail occurs at Rainy Pass. Remember that extreme weather is possible at the elevation of the pass.

Washington Pass, 5 miles after Rainy Pass and 600 feet higher, has a picnic area. Beyond this pass, the downhill is steep and you may see snow in shady spots. Mazama, a pinprick on the map 17 miles from Washington Pass, has a general store and post office.

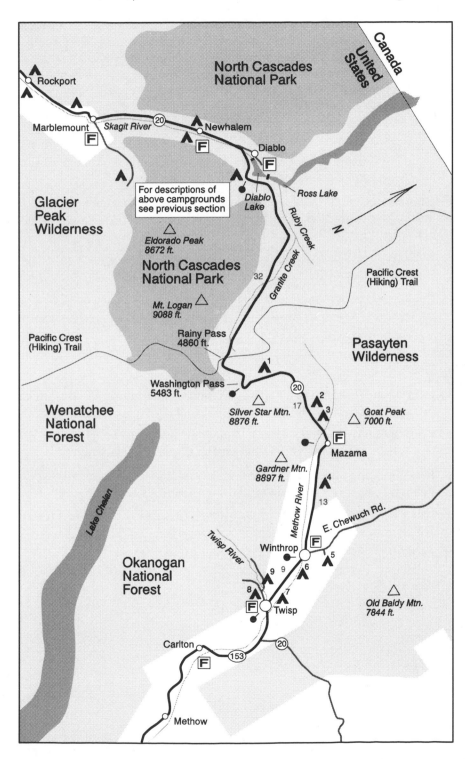

North Cascades
National Park

Canada
United States

Rockport

Marblemount
Skagit River
20
Newhalem

Diablo

Glacier
Peak
Wilderness

For descriptions of
above campgrounds
see previous section

Diablo
Lake

Ross Lake

Ruby Creek

Granite Creek

N

Eldorado Peak
8672 ft.

North Cascades
National Park

32

Pacific Crest
(Hiking) Trail

Mt. Logan
9088 ft.

Rainy Pass
4860 ft.

Pasayten
Wilderness

Pacific Crest
(Hiking) Trail

Washington Pass
5483 ft.

1

20

2

17

3

Goat Peak
7000 ft.

Wenatchee
National
Forest

Silver Star Mtn.
8876 ft.

Mazama

Gardner Mtn.
8897 ft.

4

Methow River

13

E. Chewuch Rd.

Lake Chelan

Twisp River

Winthrop

5

Okanogan
National
Forest

9

9

6

8

7

Old Baldy Mtn.
7844 ft.

Twisp

Carlton

153

20

Methow

Thirteen miles from Mazama, Winthrop is an old-west theme town with a grocery store; expect many tourists in the summer months. At this low elevation, summer high temperatures easily reach into the 90s.

From Winthrop, follow the Methow River 9 miles gently downhill on Highway 20 to Twisp, which has one grocery store. There are a number of campgrounds in the vicinity.

## Campgrounds

1. **Lone Fir Campground.** 5 miles north of Washington Pass on Highway 20. Has drinking water. Open 6/1–10/15. Forest Service.

2. **Klipchuck Campground.** 12 miles northeast of Washington Pass, then 1 mile off Highway 20. Has flush and pit toilets. Open 5/15–10/15. Forest Service.

3. **Early Winters Campground.** 14 miles northeast of Washington Pass on Highway 20. Has drinking water. Open 5/15–10/15. Forest Service.

4. **Rocking Horse Campground.** 4 miles southeast of Mazama on Highway 20. Has showers. Privately run.

5. **Pearrygin Lake State Park.** 2 miles north from Winthrop on East Chewuch Road, then 2 miles east on Bear Creek Road. Has flush and pit toilets, swimming. Open 4/1–11/30. State park.

6. **KOA Kampground.** 2 miles south of Winthrop on Highway 20. Has store, swimming, laundry, showers. Open 4/15–11/1. Privately run.

7. **River Bend Trailer Park.** 2 miles north of Twisp just off Highway 20. Has laundry, groceries, swimming. Open all year. Privately run.

8. **Paradise Valley RV Resort.** 2 miles west of Twisp via Poorman Creek Road. Has laundry, groceries, swimming. Open 5/1–10/31. Privately run.

9. **War Creek Campground.** 3 miles west of Twisp on Forest Road 44. Has drinking water. Open 5/25–9/15. Forest Service.

A stream cascades down a rocky cliff between Diablo Lake and Rainy Pass.

# Twisp
# to
# Lincoln Rock State Park

<u>79 miles</u> • Apple Orchards and the Columbia River

This relatively level stretch follows the Methow River, then the broad Columbia River, and finally enters irrigated apple and pear orchard country. Because this part of Washington is often hot during the summer, get an early start and drink plenty of liquids.

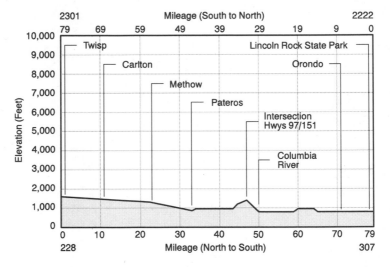

Leave Twisp on Highway 20 heading south. About 2 miles from town bear right and take Highway 153. Nine miles down the road, the town of Carlton has a store. Continue riding south on a slight downhill along the Methow River.

Near Pateros, 22 miles to the south of Carlton, is Alta Lake State Park (#1). In Pateros, turn right and proceed south on Highway 97 about 0.2 mile before turning left onto Starr Road, which parallels Highway 97. After 4 miles on Starr Road, rejoin Highway 97 and continue south approximately 10 miles to the top of a short incline. At the top, before reaching the city of Chelan, leave Highway 97 and take Highway 151.

*Just off the Trail is the Lake Chelan recreation area. Lake Chelan is a scenic, naturally-formed lake 55 miles in length and up to 1,500 feet deep. The town of Chelan (population 3,000) at the southern end of the lake has preserved some of its historic buildings.*

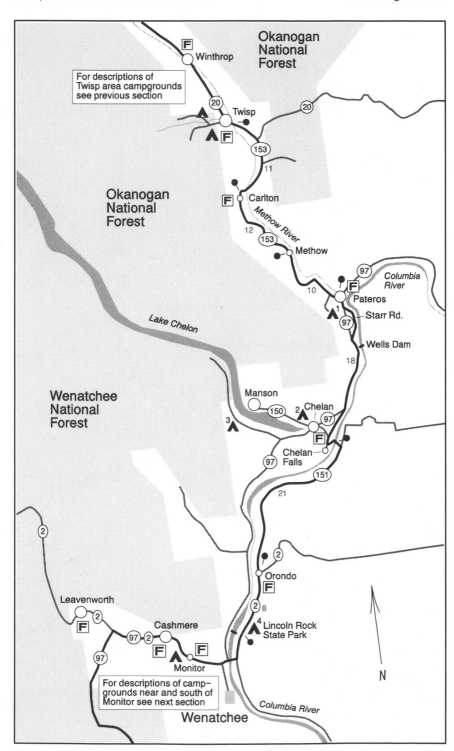

Okanogan National Forest

Winthrop

For descriptions of Twisp area campgrounds see previous section

20   Twisp

153

11

Okanogan National Forest

F   Carlton

Methow River

12

153

Methow

97   Columbia River

10

F

1   Pateros

97   Starr Rd.

Wells Dam

18

Lake Chelon

Wenatchee National Forest

Manson

150   2   Chelan

3   97

F

97   Chelan Falls

151

21

2

2   Orondo

F

Leavenworth

2   8

2   4   Lincoln Rock State Park

F

97   2   Cashmere

97   F   F

F   Monitor

For descriptions of campgrounds near and south of Monitor see next section

Columbia River

Wenatchee

N

Apple farmers working near the Columbia River.

*A passenger boat provides daily round-trip service between Chelan and the town of Stehekin on the far northern end of the lake. The boat, which operates between April 15 and October 15, leaves Chelan at 8:30 a.m., arrives at Stehekin at 12:30 p.m. and arrives back at Chelan again at 6 p.m. (with intermediate stops). In 1988 the basic fare was $18 for a round trip plus an extra $13 for a bicycle.*

*Lake Chelan State Park (#3) is located 12 miles west of Chelan. Six miles further up the same road is Twenty-Five Mile Creek State Park. If you have the time, the Lake Chelan area is worth checking out.*

Once on Highway 151, follow it downhill, passing near Chelan Falls, which has a store and lots of apple processing and storage facilities. Take the bridge across the Columbia River and follow Highway 151 south through irrigated apple and pear country. In the summer, the incessant spurt, spurt sounds of sprinklers fill the air.

Continue south on Highway 151 along the Columbia River. Twenty-one miles from the bridge over the Columbia River, Highway 151 becomes Highway 2 at Orondo, which has a store and a hamburger joint. Continue south on Highway 2.

In this area the vistas along the Columbia River Valley are stately. Ducks skitter along the surface of the river, which is heavily dammed to extract hydroelectric power and irrigation water.

Eight miles south of Orondo near Rocky Beach Dam is Lincoln Rock State Park (#4).

## Campgrounds

1. **Alta Lake State Park.** 2 miles southwest of Pateros off Highway 153. A fair climb to get to. Has showers, swimming. Open all year. State park.

2. **Lakeshore Trailer Park.** 1 mile north of Chelan on Highway 150. Has laundry. Open 3/1–11/15. Municipal park.

3. **Lake Chelan State Park.** 9 miles west of Chelan off Highway 97 and on the south side of Lake Chelan. Has swimming. Open 4/1–11/14. State park.

4. **Lincoln Rock State Park.** 6 miles south of Orondo on Highway 2. Has swimming. Open all year. State park.

# Lincoln Rock State Park
# to
# Ellensburg

<u>73 miles</u> • The Winds of Ellensburg

After continuing through orchard country near Wenatchee, the Trail climbs into Wenatchee National Forest. After a 4,000-foot pass, Highway 97 heads downhill into the dry country around Ellensburg.

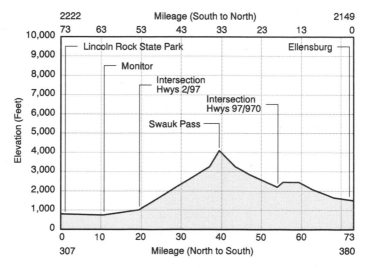

From Lincoln Rock State Park, continue south on Highway 2 for 5 miles, then turn right and take Highway 2/97 across the Columbia River toward Wenatchee and Monitor. Instead of going to Wenatchee, continue on Highway 2/97 into Monitor, which has grocery stores. Wenatchee River County Park (#1) in Monitor is a fine overnight stop.

Highway 2/97 out of Monitor has a nice wide shoulder. Nine miles northwest of Monitor, turn left to stay on Highway 97. You will soon enter Wenatchee National Forest. There are several campgrounds in this area.

Begin climbing until, 20 miles from the intersection of Highway 2 and Highway 97, you reach the crest at 4,102-foot Swauk Pass. Coasting down the other side, you will pass a restaurant.

Fifteen miles from Swauk Pass turn left, staying on Highway 97. Unfortunately, the climbing is not over for the day, but after gaining a hill, you will have a 13-mile downhill into Ellensburg. The day I rode this stretch, a strong wind literally blew my partner and I all the way into town at speeds as high as 35 mph. In this area, the lush vegetation encountered in the higher

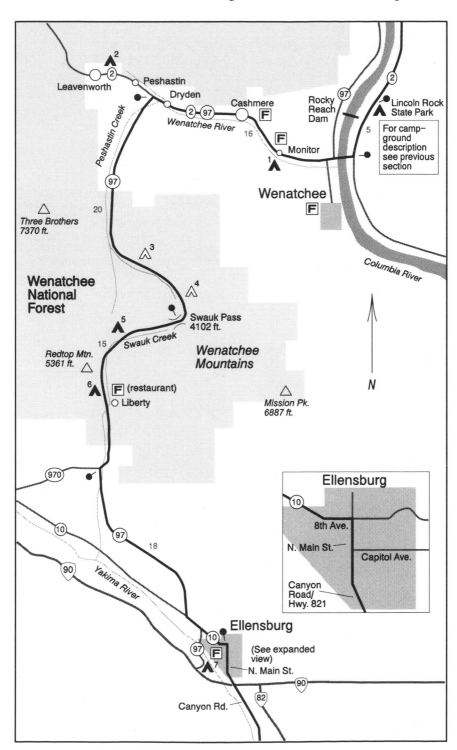

elevations has given way again to arid, nearly barren land.

As the Trail approaches Ellensburg, Highway 97 joins with Highway 10. Shortly thereafter, continue going straight on Highway 10 as Highway 97 veers off to the right. Highway 10 becomes 8$^{th}$ Avenue. Ellensburg has a population of 13,000 and 6 motels. There is also a KOA campground and a well-equipped bicycle shop.

## Campgrounds

1. **Wenatchee River County Park.** In Monitor adjacent to Highway 2/97. Has showers, grocery store across street. Open 4/1–9/30. County park.

2. **Pine Village KOA Kampground.** 4 miles west of intersection of Highway 97 and Highway 2 on Highway 2, then 0.5 mile north on River Bend Drive. Has store, laundry, heated pool. Open 4/1–11/1. Privately run.

3. **Bonanza Campground.** On Highway 97, 15 miles south of intersection of Highway 2 and Highway 97, and 5 miles north of Swauk Pass. Has no drinking water, but creek water can be purified. Open 4/15–11/30. Forest Service.

4. **Tronson Creek Campground.** On Highway 97, just north of Swauk Pass. Has no drinking water. Open 5/15–10/30. Forest Service.

5. **Swauk Campground.** On Highway 97, 4 miles southwest of Swauk Pass. Has flush and pit toilets. Open 4/15–11/30. Forest Service.

6. **Mineral Springs Campground.** On Highway 97, 10 miles south of Swauk Pass and 1 mile north of Liberty. Has drinking water. Open 4/15–11/30. Forest Service.

7. **KOA Kampground.** West of Ellensburg near intersection of Freeway 90 and Highway 97. Has store, laundry, pool, showers. Open 4/1–10/15. Privately run.

The summit of Swauk Pass between Monitor and Ellensburg is a welcome sight.

# Ellensburg
# to
# Rimrock Lake

73 miles  •  A Beautiful River Canyon

This section follows the picturesque and winding Yakima River Canyon for approximately 25 miles, then traverses a quaint rural area between Selah and Naches before heading up a breezy canyon to Rimrock Lake.

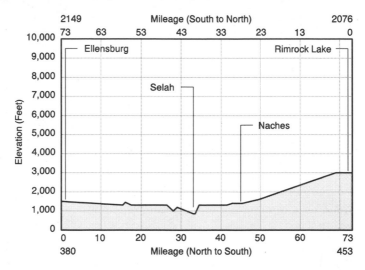

Take Main Street south in Ellensburg. Main Street becomes Canyon Road, which crosses under Freeway 90, and becomes Highway 821. Enter the beautiful and isolated (because nearby Freeway 82 carries most of the traffic) Yakima River Canyon with its many twists and turns. The canyon is geologically interesting with exposed formations of volcanically-laid basalt. In addition to Riverview Campground (#1), there are many places in the canyon which have camping possibilities, although there are no toilets.

About 30 miles from Ellensburg, turn right onto Harrison Road. Two miles beyond turn left onto Wenas Road and ride into the prosperous town of Selah. You may want to stop at the large supermarket on the outskirts of town.

In Selah, turn right onto Bartlett Avenue, then left onto North 1st Street, and then right onto Fremont. Bicycle 2 miles west on Fremont (it becomes Pleasant Hill Road) before turning left onto Selah Heights Road. Go one block, turn right onto Maple Way, and travel a mile before turning right onto Old Naches Highway. Follow Old Naches Highway (black arrow signs point the way) into Naches where it becomes 2nd Street. In Naches, turn left onto

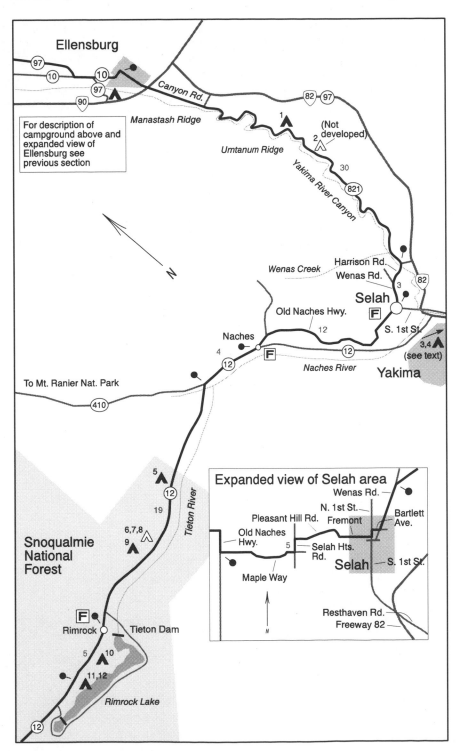

Ellensburg

97
10
10
97
90
Canyon Rd.

82 — 97

Manastash Ridge

For description of
campground above and
expanded view of
Ellensburg see
previous section

Umtanum Ridge

(Not
developed)

1

2

Yakima River Canyon

30

821

N

Harrison Rd.

Wenas Creek

Wenas Rd.

3

82

Selah

F

Old Naches Hwy.

12

S. 1st St.

Naches

4

12

F

Naches River

3,4
(see text)

Yakima

To Mt. Ranier Nat. Park

410

5

12

Tieton River

19

6,7,8

9

Snoqualmie
National
Forest

**Expanded view of Selah area**

Wenas Rd.

N. 1st St.

Pleasant Hill Rd.

Fremont

Bartlett
Ave.

Old Naches
Hwy.

5

Selah Hts.
Rd.

Selah

S. 1st St.

Maple Way

N

Resthaven Rd.

Freeway 82

F

Rimrock

Tieton Dam

5

10

11,12

Rimrock Lake

12

Canal Street (not shown on map), bike two blocks, and turn right onto Highway 12. The distance between Selah and Naches is 12 miles.

Four miles beyond Naches, make sure you turn left and continue west on Highway 12 rather than going straight on Highway 410. You will be climbing gradually up the Tieton River Valley (here I ran into the strongest headwinds I have encountered anywhere on the Trail). Trees become more numerous as the elevation increases. About 22 miles from Naches, just before arriving at Rimrock Lake, is a grocery store. The lake, created by a dam, is quite picturesque with many boats moored along its shore.

At this 3,000-foot elevation, my partner and I shivered through an overnight freeze in Indian Creek Campground (#12) in August and we saw a coyote.

### Campgrounds

1. **Riverview Campground.** 13 miles south of Ellensburg on Highway 821. Privately run.

2. **Impromptu Campground.** 19 miles south of Ellensburg on Highway 821.

   *The exact locations of campgrounds #3 and #4 are not shown on the map. To reach them from the city of Selah, take 1st Street south over the Yakima River and Freeway 82. Here, 1st Street becomes Resthaven Road. Bike 2 miles on Resthaven Road, turn right onto Marsh Road, bike about 1 mile, turn right onto Butterfield, turn left onto Terrace Heights Road, turn right onto Keyes Road, and bike 1 mile to the entrance road for Yakima Sportsman State Park or 2 miles to the Yakima KOA.*

3. **Yakima Sportsman State Park.** Has flush and pit toilets. Open all year. State Park.

4. **Yakima KOA.** Has laundry, store, swimming. Open all year. Privately run.

5. **Windy Point Campground.** 12 miles west of Naches on Highway 12. Has drinking water. Open 4/1–11/18. Forest Service.

6. **Willows Campground.** 18 miles west of Naches on Highway 12. Has no drinking water. Open 5/25–9/16. Forest Service.

7. **Wild Rose Campground.** 19 miles west of Naches on Highway 12. Open 4/1–11/18. Forest Service.

8. **River Bend Campground.** 20 miles west of Naches on Highway 12. Open 5/22–9/14. Forest Service.

9. **Hause Creek Campground.** 20 miles west of Naches on Highway 12. Has drinking water. Open 5/24–11/18. Forest Service.

10. **Silver Cove Resort.** On Rimrock Lake, 2 miles west of town of Rimrock on Highway 12. Has camping, restaurant. Open all year. Privately run.

11. **Rimrock Lake Resort.** On Rimrock Lake, 5 miles west of Rimrock on Highway 12. Has restaurant. Privately run.

12. **Indian Creek Campground.** On Rimrock Lake, 5 miles west of Rimrock on Highway 12. Has drinking water, swimming. Open 5/24–9/16. Forest Service.

The long and winding Yakima River Canyon south of Ellensburg.

# Rimrock Lake
# to
# Council Lake

Includes an alternate route near Mount St. Helens.

## 72 miles • Volcano Country

Prepare to enter a remote, forested, upland area between Mt. Adams and the famous Mount St. Helens volcano. After climbing to 4,500-foot White Pass, the Trail passes down the Cowlitz River Valley to Randle, the jumping off point for either the main route close to Mt. Adams or the longer, alternate route near Mount St. Helens. On the alternate route there is also a side trip to Windy Ridge Overlook which affords the best views of Mount St. Helens. There are stretches of unpaved road along both routes.

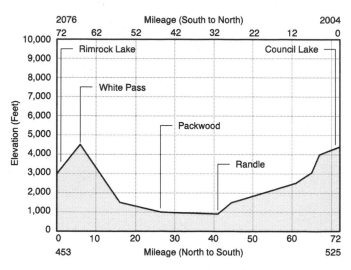

As you proceed up toward 4,500-foot White Pass on Highway 12 from Rimrock Lake, the road has wide shoulders, but they diminish near the crest. At the crest, 7 miles from Indian Creek Campground at Rimrock Lake, is a crossing of The Pacific Crest (Hiking) Trail. On the other side of White Pass are some excellent views, weather permitting, of the snow-capped, 14,410-foot Mt. Rainier volcano. Be careful on the downhill, which is long and sometimes steep. This entire area is well-forested and beautiful.

About 21 miles beyond White Pass is the town of Packwood with stores and a ranger station, which has maps and information. From Packwood, bicycle down the Cowlitz River Valley on Highway 12 another 18 miles to Randle, which has a grocery store. You may wish to stock up on food because there are no stores on the main route between Randle and Trout Lake.

In Randle, you must decide whether you wish to take the main route near Mt. Adams or the alternate route near Mount St. Helens. You may wish to check at the Randle Ranger Station because there is frequent road work in the area between Randle and the Columbia River.

The map for this area includes all important roads between Randle and the Columbia River. The map indicates whether roads are paved or not. Unpaved roads in this area are hard packed and fairly easy to ride on, but occasionally fresh-laid gravel can make biking difficult.

*If you wish to make the side trip to Mount St. Helens refer to the Mount St. Helens alternate route later in this section. A higher percentage of roads on the Mount St. Helens alternate route are paved, but the route is longer by 30 miles and has more climbing. However, it should be noted that, weather permitting, the main route will afford only a very distant glimpse of famous Mount St. Helens.*

Mount St. Helens as seen from the southeast along Road 25.

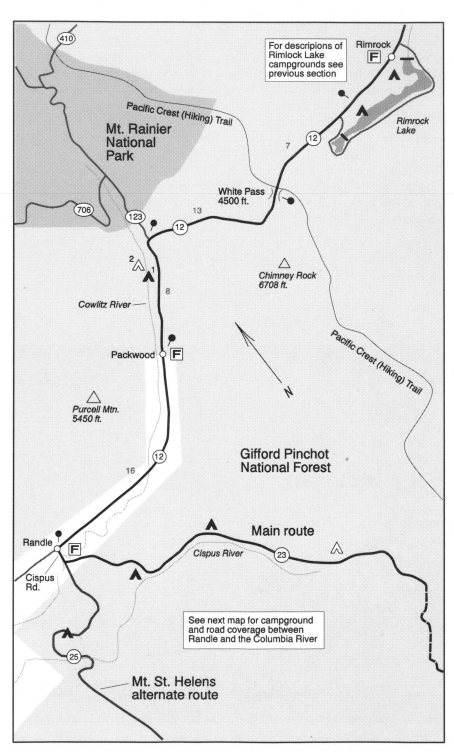

410

For descriptions of
Rimlock Lake
campgrounds see
previous section

Rimrock
F

Pacific Crest (Hiking) Trail

Mt. Rainier
National
Park

Rimrock
Lake

12

7

706

123

White Pass
4500 ft.

13

12

2

1

Chimney Rock
6708 ft.

8

Cowlitz River

Packwood  F

N

Pacific Crest (Hiking) Trail

Purcell Mtn.
5450 ft.

12

16

Gifford Pinchot
National Forest

Main route

Randle  F

Cispus River

23

Cispus
Rd.

See next map for campground
and road coverage between
Randle and the Columbia River

25

Mt. St. Helens
alternate route

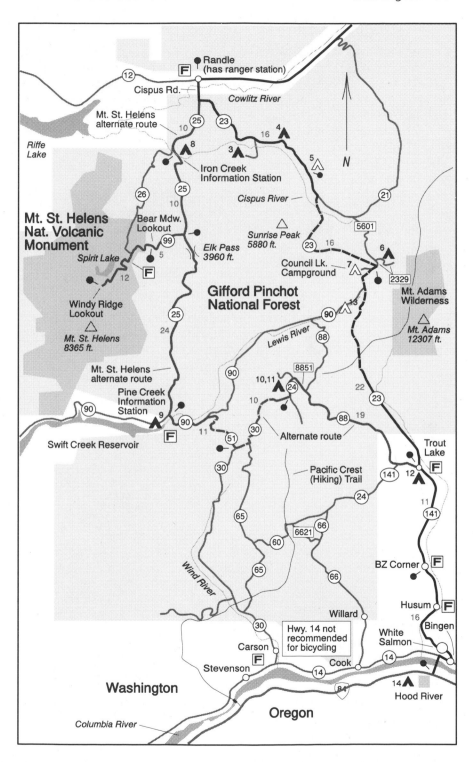

## Continuing on the main route

To use the main route, depart from Highway 12 at Randle and head south on Cispus Road for about 1 mile before turning left onto two-lane, paved Forest Road 23 and entering Gifford Pinchot National Forest. The paved portion of this road was one of the most beautiful, quiet roads I encountered in all of Washington and Oregon.

Approximately 18 miles from the intersection of Cispus Road and Forest Road 23 and 3 miles past Blue Lake Creek Campground (#5), the paved road comes to a "Y" with a paved road continuing to the left and an unpaved road splitting off to the right. Take the unpaved road to the right.

Approximately 11 miles from the beginning of the unpaved road and after some climbing, a plateau of sorts is reached at an altitude of 4,300 feet. At this point, Council Lake is about one mile off the main route to the west. The campground there has no drinking water so boiling or chemically treating the lake water before drinking is a must.

## Mount St. Helens alternate route

The Mount St. Helens alternate route from Randle to Trout Lake is 83 miles. Add another 32 miles if you wish to make the round trip to Windy Ridge Overlook for the best view of Mount St. Helens. This route is entirely paved with the exception of 15 miles.

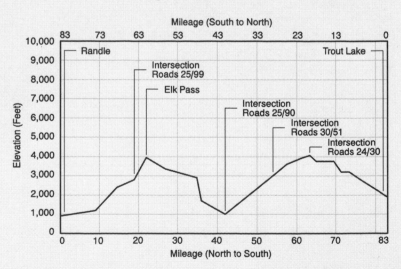

Travel south from Randle on Cispus Road for 1 mile and then continue south on Forest Road 25 through an area with both deciduous and evergreen trees. Ten miles from Randle is Iron Creek Campground (#8) and an information center with maps and information about Mount St. Helens and road conditions. Shortly after the campground, begin climbing. The paved road surface is excellent although there are no paved shoulders.

Ten miles from Iron Creek Campground (#8) and after a 1,650-foot elevation gain you reach the intersection of Forest Road 25 and Forest Road 99.

*To get the best views of Mount St. Helens, which erupted spec-tacularly in 1980, take the side trip on Forest Road 99. The 16-mile road is excellent and paved all the way to its end at Windy Ridge Overlook. But you will work for the view! Referring to the special elevation profile for Forest Road 99, there is a 5-mile, 1,000-foot climb to the Bear Meadow Overlook, which has pit toilets. This vantage point offers a fine enough view for many.*

### Forest Road 99 to Windy Ridge Overlook

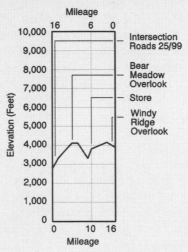

*After Bear Meadow, the thousands of trees felled by the eruption come into view. Six miles from Bear Meadow Overlook is a store and restaurant. The end of the road is 6 miles from the restaurant and a mere 4 miles from the lava dome inside the remains of Mount St. Helens. The ride on Forest Road 99 can be windy and cold, but the impressions of the power of an eruption make the ride unfor-gettable.*

Continuing south on Forest Road 25 from the intersection of Forest Roads 25 and 99, climb for 4 more miles to the crest at Elk Pass. Because of extensive logging in the area, keep an eye out for heavy trucks. Forest Road 25 has a few short gravel spots as it heads downhill along the top of a long ridge. There are several good views of Mount St. Helens on the route. At the bottom of the ridge, some 15 miles from Elk Pass, is a bridge over the Muddy River. This is one of the locations where fast mud flows from the Mount St. Helens eruption passed through. Information boards tell the full story.

Continue south on Forest Road 25 from the Muddy River bridge for 5 miles until you reach Pine Creek Information Station on Swift Reservoir, which has pit toilets. Nearby is Swift Campground (#9). Now turn left onto Forest Road 90 and cross the Lewis River, which marks the end of your downhill travel. On the other side is a grocery store and rustic motel.

Continue biking 5 miles on paved Forest Road 90 before making a right turn onto gravel-surfaced Forest Road 51. Bike uphill, initially on a series of switchbacks, for 6 miles and then turn left onto paved Forest Road 30. You will have passed Outlaw Ridge Observation Point on Forest Road 51 which has pit toilets and a view of Mount St. Helens.

Two miles from Forest Road 51, at a "Y" in the road (not shown on map), Forest Road 30 becomes hard-packed gravel. Bear right at the "Y," staying on Forest Road 30, and bike gradually uphill. Two miles from the "Y," turn left at the intersection with Forest Road 65, and remain on Forest Road 30, but now heading north. There is much clear-cut logging in this area. After 6 miles of hard-packed gravel, the paved road begins again. After about 1 mile on paved Forest Road 30, turn left onto paved Forest Road 24. The turnoff for South Campground (#10) is 1 mile ahead and the turnoff for Tillicum Campground (#11) is 2 miles ahead. The remainder of the road to Trout Lake is generally downhill.

Three miles from the intersection of Forest Road 30 and Forest Road 24 turn right onto Forest Road 8851 near Big Mosquito Lake, and head southeast toward Trout Lake. The Pacific Crest (Hiking) Trail crosses nearby. After 3 miles, Forest Road 8851 joins Forest Road 88. Continue straight (heading southeast) on Forest Road 88 in the direction of Trout Lake. Now the road widens and there is some up and down work. Twelve miles from the intersection of Forest Road 8851 and Forest Road 88 turn left onto Highway 141 and ride a short distance into the town of Trout Lake. Ah, civilization again!

Trout Lake has a store, a restaurant, a county park with camping facilities, several bed and breakfast places, an inn, and a ranger station.

*To continue from Trout Lake, pick up the main route mid-way in the next section between Council Lake and Hood River, Oregon.*

## Campgrounds

1. **La Wis Wis Campground.** Off Highway 12, 1 mile southwest of intersection of Highway 12 and Highway 123, then 0.5 mile on Forest Road 1272. Has flush and pit toilets. Open 5/21–9/20. Forest service.

2. **Hatchery RV Campground.** 0.2 mile further down Forest Road 1272 from campground #1. Has no drinking water. 5/21–9/20. Forest Service.

3. **Tower Rock Campground.** 8 miles southeast of Randle on Forest Road 23, then 2 miles south on Forest Road 28, then 2 miles west on Forest Road 76. Has drinking water. Open 5/15–9/30. Forest Service.

4. **North Fork Campground.** 11 miles southeast of Randle on Forest Road 23. Has drinking water. Open 5/15–9/30. Forest Service.

5. **Blue Lake Creek Campground.** 16 miles southeast of Randle on Forest Road 23. Has no drinking water. Forest Service.

6. **Takhlakh Campground.** 32 miles southeast of Randle on Forest Road 23, then 2 miles north on Forest Road 2329. Has drinking water. Another campground, Olallie Lake Campground, is nearby but has no drinking water. Open 6/15–9/30. Forest Service.

7. **Council Lake Campground.** 32 miles southeast of Randle on Forest Road 23, then 1 mile west on Forest Road 2334. Has no drinking water, but lake water can be purified. Open 7/1–9/15. Forest Service.

8. **Iron Creek Campground.** 9 miles south of Randle on Forest Road 25. Has drinking water. Open 5/15–10/30. Forest Service.

9. **Swift Campground.** On Highway 90 at Swift Reservoir, 2 miles southwest of the intersection of Forest Road 90 and Forest Road 25. Has drinking water, swimming, nearby store. Pacific Power and Light.

10. **South Campground.** Off Forest Road 24, 1 mile north of the intersection of Forest Road 30 and Forest Road 24. Location may not be signed. Has drinking water. Open 6/15–9/30. Forest Service.

11. **Tillicum Campground.** Off Forest Road 24, 2 miles north of the intersection of Forest Road 30 and Forest Road 24. Has drinking water. Open 6/15–9/30. Forest Service.

12. **Guler-Mt. Adams County Park.** In the city of Trout Lake. Has flush toilets, pay showers, nearby store. County park.

# Council Lake
# to
# Hood River, OR

*Use map on page 51 in previous section.*

### 49 miles • A Piece of Cake

See this easy section as a reward for finishing the state of Washington. The Trail heads downhill through forested land to Trout Lake, then downhill some more through more populated areas to the cities of White Salmon and Bingen. Finally, you cross the broad Columbia River on an old bridge.

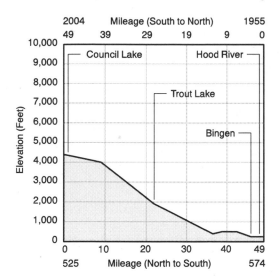

Forest Service maps of this area show a profusion of roads, but they are very well signed and sticking to the route should not be a problem. If you went to Council Lake, return to Forest Road 23, head south again, and cross a bridge after 0.6 mile.

The hard-packed gravel road continues for approximately 2 miles beyond the Council Lake turnoff before a short section of pavement begins. But don't get your hopes up — it lasts only a quarter mile. The road has a gradual downhill grade.

Riding Road 23 north of Council Lake in Washington.

About 5 miles from the Council Lake turnoff, there is a brief view through a gap in the trees of 8,400-foot Mount St. Helens. The volcano is 28 miles to the west and good weather is needed to see it. Mt. Adams, the nearby 12,307-foot volcano to the east, is dormant.

Eight and one-half miles from the viewpoint, pavement begins which continues all the way to the Columbia River. Continue on Forest Road 23 to the town of Trout Lake, which is 2,500 feet lower than Council Lake. Trout Lake has a county park with camping facilities, a store, a restaurant, several bed and breakfast places, and a ranger station.

*The Mount St. Helens alternate route intersects the main route here.*

In Trout Lake, head south on Highway 141 toward the city of White Salmon. Eleven miles from Trout Lake is the town of BZ Corner with a grocery store and restaurant. A few miles further down Highway 141 is the town of Husum with a cafe and bed and breakfast place. At this point, you will probably get your first views of Mt. Hood to the south in Oregon.

Enter White Salmon on Highway 141. White Salmon is a busy, German-motif, touristy place. The downhill in White Salmon is rather steep, leveling off at the town of Bingen on the Columbia River. In Bingen, turn right onto Highway 14, then turn left and take the old and narrow Hood River Toll Bridge into Oregon. When you ride it you can look down through vertical metal slats to the water below — disconcerting, to say the least. There is an information center on the Oregon end of the bridge, a bicycle shop in the city of Hood River, and Viento State Park (#14) is just off Freeway 84, 8 miles to the west.

In Oregon, bicycling on the shoulder of freeways is permitted except in Portland. Now there is a progressive state! I should mention that in the summer in Washington and Oregon there is an abundance of wild blackberries, although those near roads have probably been sprayed with chemicals and should not be eaten.

## Campgrounds

12. **Guler-Mt. Adams County Park.** In the city of Trout Lake. Has flush toilets, pay showers. Store nearby. County park.

13. **Twin Falls Campground.** 2 miles south of Council Lake on Forest Road 23, then 2 miles southwest on Forest Road 90, then a short distance south. Has no drinking water, but water from the Lewis River can be purified. Forest Service.

14. **Viento State Park.** Just off Freeway 84, 8 miles west of the city of Hood River. Has drinking water. Open 4/15–10/31. State park.

# Region 2
# Oregon

Vapor trails entwine above an early morning campsite.

# Hood River
# to
# Clackamas Lake

<u>59 miles</u> • Into Cascades Backcountry

A long and steady climb up and around 11,235-foot Mt. Hood dominates this mostly-forested portion of the Trail, which ends at the 3,000-foot level in a lake area with many campgrounds.

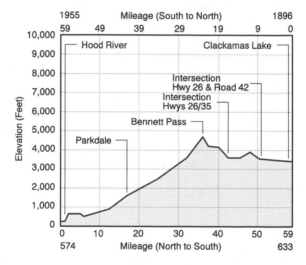

*Highway 35 is a more direct route south, but the described route is more interesting, less-travelled, and more relaxing — except for a short, steep section in the city of Hood River.*

If you are coming off the Columbia River bridge from the state of Washington and intend to continue bicycling south toward Mt. Hood, bicycle directly off the bridge to a stop sign. Turn right and head west towards a marina. At the Hood River Museum, walk your bike across the pedestrian bridge, then turn left and proceed south on the freeway overpass (freeway exit #63) onto 2$^{nd}$ Street and into the city of Hood River.

At the first stop sign in the city of Hood River, turn right onto Oak Street (Highway 30) and bike 9 blocks to the flashing yellow light at 13$^{th}$ Street. Turn left onto 13$^{th}$ Street and head up a short, steep grade which will probably require you to walk your bike. Thirteenth Street soon becomes 12$^{th}$ Street, which in turn becomes Tucker Road and Highway 281. Continue on Tucker Road and Highway 281.

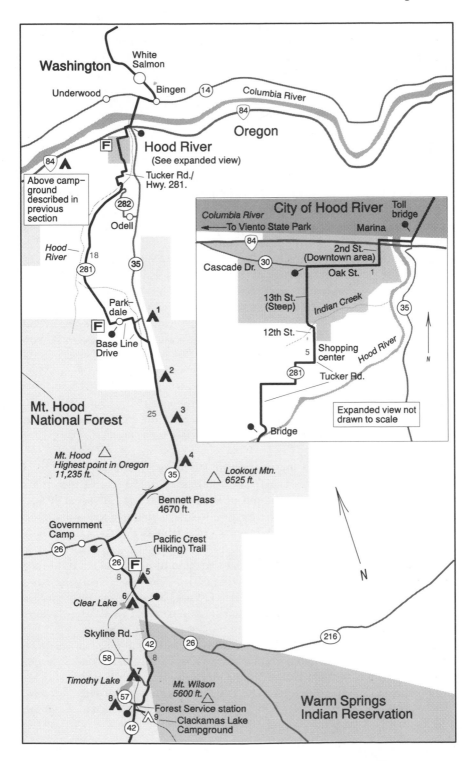

Washington

White Salmon

Bingen  (14)    Columbia River

Underwood

(84)

Oregon

F  Hood River
(See expanded view)

(84)  ▲
Above camp-
ground
described in
previous
section

Tucker Rd./
Hwy. 281.

(282)

Odell

Hood
River    18

(281)    (35)

Park-
dale

F

Base Line
Drive

▲1

▲2

Mt. Hood
National Forest    25    ▲3

Mt. Hood  △
Highest point in Oregon
11,235 ft.

▲4

(35)    △  Lookout Mtn.
6525 ft.

Bennett Pass
4670 ft.

Government
Camp

(26)

Pacific Crest
(Hiking) Trail

(26)  F
8    ▲5

Clear Lake  6    ▲

Skyline Rd.

(42)    (26)

(58)    8

Timothy Lake    ▲7

8  (57)    Mt. Wilson
▲    5600 ft.  △

Forest Service station

(42)    △9  Clackamas Lake
Campground

(216)

Warm Springs
Indian Reservation

N

### City of Hood River

Columbia River
←To Viento State Park    Marina    Toll
bridge

(84)

2nd St.
(Downtown area)

Cascade Dr.    (30)

Oak St.    1

13th St.
(Steep)    Indian Creek

12th St.

5    Shopping
center    Hood River    (35)

(281)    Tucker Rd.

N

Bridge

Expanded view not
drawn to scale

*If you are coming from Viento State Park, heading east on Freeway 84,
take exit #62, the Westcliff exit, and travel about a mile on Cascade
Drive (Highway 30) to the flashing yellow light at 13$^{th}$ Street. Turn
right onto 13$^{th}$ Street and join the route described above and below.*

At the top of the grade, 0.8 mile from Oak Street, there is a shopping
center. From the shopping center follow the Highway 281 signs for 4 miles
to a bridge over the Hood River. This is a pretty, mostly-wooded area. After
the bridge bear to the right to stay on Highway 281; do not follow Highway
282 toward Odell.

Some maps show a town called Dee about 6 miles from the intersection
of Highway 281 and Highway 282. All you will find there is a large lumber
mill. From the mill, continue south on Highway 281 for 5 miles to Parkdale.
At Parkdale, which has a grocery store, turn left onto Base Line Drive and
follow it for 3 miles as it makes a turn to the right, near Toll Bridge
Campground (#1), and connects with Highway 35. Continue south on Highway 35, which in this area has an excellent surface and wide shoulder.

Mt. Hood now dominates the skyline as the Trail circles and climbs around
its eastern flank. About 4 miles from the intersection of Base Line Drive and
Highway 35 is Routson Park Campground (#2); 4 miles beyond is Sherwood
Campground (#3); 4 miles beyond that is Robinhood Campground (#4). You
will pass the entrance to Mt. Hood Meadows Ski Area just before reaching
the summit of Bennett Pass at 4,670 feet. This area is lushly wooded. After
several miles of downhill riding the terrain levels out a bit.

Six miles from Bennett Pass, turn left off Highway 35 onto busy Highway
26 and bike south. Three miles from the intersection of Highway 35 and
Highway 26 is a gas station and small grocery store, strategically placed for
hungry and thirsty cyclists.

About 5 miles from the intersection of Highway 35 and Highway 26 is
Frog Lake Campground (#5) near Wapinitia Pass at 3,950 feet. A few miles
more down Highway 26 is the summit of Blue Box Pass at 4,024 feet. These
are insignificant passes, though being able to claim you crossed so many in
a single day may give your ego a boost. Just past Blue Box Pass is the turnoff
for Clear Lake Campground (#6).

About a mile after the Clear Lake Campground turnoff, make a right turn
from Highway 26 onto Skyline Road (also called Forest Road 42) and head
toward Timothy Lake. The Pacific Crest (Hiking) Trail passes through this
area. Also, you will be passing through a small portion of the Warm Springs
Indian Reservation.

There is a turnoff to Little Crater Campground (#7) about 4 miles from
Highway 26. Four miles later, you can turn right onto Forest Road 57 to go
to the campgrounds (#8) at Timothy Lake, or turn left and head south (staying
on Forest Road 42) to continue on the Trail in the direction of Detroit Lake.
Just south of the intersection of Forest Road 57 and Forest Road 42 is the
turnoff for Clackamas Lake Campground (#9).

During one August, I encountered early morning temperatures near freezing at Clackamas Lake (elevation 3,400 feet). I also encountered mosquitoes in this area.

## Campgrounds

1. **Toll Bridge Campground.** On Toll Bridge Road between Base Line Drive and Highway 35, and east of Parkdale. Has showers. Open 4/1–10/31. County park.

2. **Routson Campground.** 7 miles south of Parkdale on Highway 35. Has drinking water, swimming. Open 5/25–10/15. County park.

3. **Sherwood Campground.** 11 miles south of Parkdale on Highway 35. Has drinking water. Open 5/15–10/15. Forest Service.

4. **Robinhood Campground.** 15 miles south of Parkdale on Highway 35. Has drinking water, swimming. Open 5/25–10/15. Forest Service.

5. **Frog Lake Campground.** On Highway 26, 5 miles south of the intersection of Highway 35 and Highway 26. Has drinking water, swimming. Open 5/15–10/1. Forest Service.

6. **Clear Lake Campground.** Turn off Highway 26 six miles south of the intersection of Highway 35 and Highway 26, then bike 0.8 mile south on Forest Road 2630, then 0.6 mile south on Forest Road 220. Has drinking water, swimming. Open 5/15–10/1. Forest Service.

7. **Little Crater Campground.** 4 miles south of Highway 26 on Forest Road 42, then 2 miles west on Forest Road 58, then a short distance west on Forest Road 230. Has drinking water. Open 5/15–10/1. Forest Service.

8. **Hood View, Gone Creek, and Oak Fork campgrounds.** All are located on the south side of Timothy Lake. Follow Forest Road 42 about 8 miles from Highway 26, then 1 to 3 miles west on Forest Road 57. All have drinking water, swimming. Open 5/15–9/15. Forest Service.

9. **Clackamas Lake Campground.** 8 miles south of Highway 26 on Forest Road 42, then 0.5 mile east on Forest Road 4270. Has no drinking water, although water is available at outside faucet at nearby Forest Service building on Forest Road 42. Has swimming. Open 5/15–10/1. Forest Service.

# Clackamas Lake
# to
# Suttle Lake

90 miles • One Long Pull at the End

After some hilly backcountry riding through national forest land and deer country, the Trail passes through the Detroit Lake resort area, over 3,817-foot Santiam Pass, and down to cozy Suttle Lake. All roads in this section are paved.

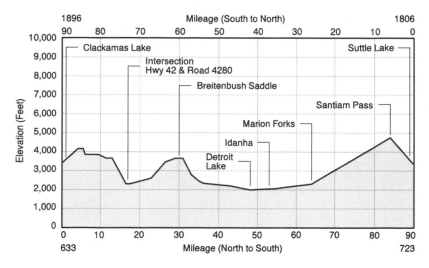

From Clackamas Lake continue biking south on Forest Road 42. The going is generally uphill for the first 4 to 5 miles, then it is downhill as the road narrows and gets rougher, though it is still paved. There are deer in this area, along with logging and clear-cutting.

Seventeen miles from Clackamas Lake, at the end of the downhill, you will intersect Forest Road 4280 at a "T" intersection. To the left, Forest Road 4280 is graveled — do not take it. Instead, turn right toward Estacada onto paved Forest Road 4280 and bike 1 mile before turning left onto Forest Road 46 toward Breitenbush Hot Springs and Detroit Lake. Here, the Clackamas River flows alongside Forest Road 46. As you travel south from here through sometimes dense forest you will have some good straight-ahead views of 10,497-foot Mt. Jefferson.

After the intersection of Forest Road 4280 and Forest Road 46, begin a climb which levels off after 10 miles. Three miles later, you will reach Breitenbush Saddle at 3,570 feet. Here, begin a steep downgrade which lasts

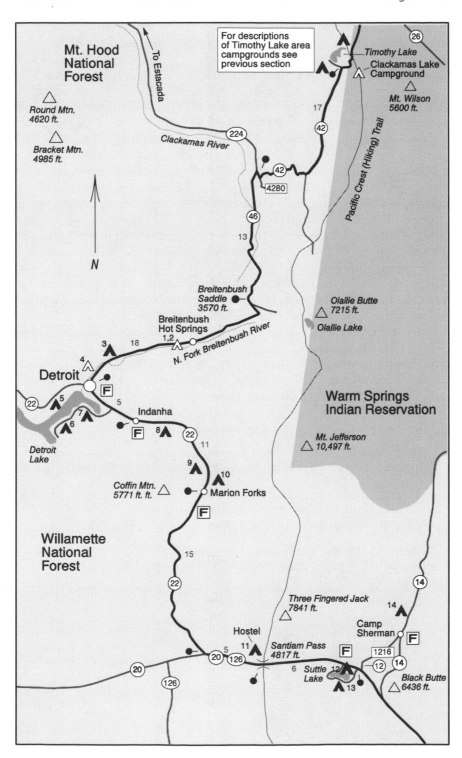

Mt. Hood National Forest

To Estacada

For descriptions of Timothy Lake area campgrounds see previous section

Timothy Lake

26

Clackamas Lake Campground

Mt. Wilson 5600 ft.

Round Mtn. 4620 ft.

Bracket Mtn. 4985 ft.

17

42

Clackamas River

224

42

4280

N

46

13

Pacific Crest (Hiking) Trail

Breitenbush Saddle 3570 ft.

Olallie Butte 7215 ft.

Breitenbush Hot Springs

1,2

Olallie Lake

N. Fork Breitenbush River

3

18

Detroit

4

F

22

5

Warm Springs Indian Reservation

Indanha

5

F

8

22

Mt. Jefferson 10,497 ft.

7

6

11

Detroit Lake

9

10

Coffin Mtn. 5771 ft. ft.

Marion Forks

F

Willamette National Forest

15

22

Three Fingered Jack 7841 ft.

14

14

Camp Sherman

F

Hostel

11

Santiam Pass 4817 ft.

F

1216

20

126

5

6

12

14

20

Suttle Lake

Black Butte 6436 ft.

126

13

3 miles before becoming more gradual. There is evidence of impromptu campsites as you gradually descend along the North Fork of the Breitenbush River.

Approximately 7 miles from Breitenbush Saddle are Breitenbush Hot Springs, Breitenbush Campground (#1), and Cleator Bend Campground (#2). Five miles later is Humbug Campground (#3). The road is excellent in this area. Five miles from Humbug Campground is the resort town of Detroit on Detroit Lake. Detroit has motels, restaurants and a grocery store.

In Detroit, turn left onto Highway 22 and head toward the cities of Sisters and Bend. Soon, begin a gradual upgrade. Three miles from Detroit is the turnoff for Southshore Campground (#6) and Hoover Campground (#7); 6 miles later is Whispering Falls Campground (#8); and 9 miles beyond that is Riverside Campground (#9).

The shoulder on Highway 22 varies from nice to nothing. Continue uphill. Two miles from Riverside Campground, at an elevation of 2,500 feet, is a store and a phone.

Fourteen miles from the store is the intersection of Highway 22 and Highway 20/126, along with a phone and a sign announcing "Alternate Bikecentennial Bike Route." Turn left and head east on Highway 20/126 for 5 miles to Santiam Pass, an American Youth Hostel, and a crossing of the Pacific Crest (Hiking) Trail.

After the summit, ride 6 miles downhill to Suttle Lake. Suttle Lake Resort has a store/restaurant and swimming. Also, there are many Forest Service campgrounds in the immediate area.

## Campgrounds

1. **Breitenbush Campground.** 10 miles northeast of Detroit on Forest Road 46. Has swimming but no drinking water. Open 5/25–9/30. Forest Service.

2. **Cleator Bend Campground.** 9 miles northeast of Detroit on Forest Road 46. Has no drinking water. Open 5/15–9/30. Forest Service.

3. **Humbug Campground.** 5 miles northeast of Detroit on Forest Road 46. Has drinking water. Open 4/15–9/30. Forest Service.

4. **Upper Arm Campground.** A very small campground with no entrance sign located 0.5 mile northeast of Detroit on Forest Road 46. Has no drinking water. Open 4/15–12/31. Forest Service.

5. **Detroit Lake State Park.** 2 miles southwest of Detroit on Highway 22 (north side of lake). Has drinking water, swimming. Open 4/15– 11/30. State park.

6. **Southshore Campground.** 3 miles southeast of Detroit on Highway 22, then 4 miles west on Forest Road 10. Has drinking water, swimming. Open 4/15–9/30. Forest Service.

7. **Hoover Campground.** 3 miles southeast of Detroit on Highway 22, then 1 mile west on Forest Road 10. Has flush toilets, swimming. Open 4/15–10/15. Forest Service.

8. **Whispering Falls Campground.** 4 miles east of Idanha on Highway 22. Has drinking water. Open 4/15–9/30. Forest Service.

9. **Riverside Campground.** 10 miles southeast of Idanha on Highway 22. Has drinking water. Open 5/15–9/30. Forest Service.

10. **Marion Forks Campground.** Several miles south of campground #9 on Highway 22; next to Marion Forks Fish Hatchery; two separate areas. Has drinking water. Open 5/15–9/15. Forest Service.

11. **American Youth Hostel.** At the top of Santiam Pass.

12. **Suttle Lake Resort.** 15 miles northwest of Sisters off Highway 20/126. Has showers, swimming, grocery store and restaurant. Privately run.

13. **Blue Bay, South Shore, and Link Creek campgrounds.** All on south side of Suttle Lake. Turnoff is 14 miles northwest of Sisters on Highway 20/126. All have drinking water, swimming. Open 4/15–10/15. Forest Service.

14. **Camp Sherman, Allingham, Smiling River, Pine Rest, and Gorge campgrounds.** Camp Sherman, which has a store, is 6 miles east of Santiam Pass on Highway 20/126, then 1 mile north on Forest Road 12, then 4 miles northeast on Forest Road 1216. Other campgrounds are 0.5 to 2 miles further north on Forest Road 14. All have drinking water. Open 5/1–10/1. Forest Service.

# Suttle Lake
# to
# Davis Lake

> *Includes a backcountry shortcut from Sisters to the Mt. Bachelor area.*

## 97 miles • Beautiful Lake Country

As you take a breather on the dry flats between the cities of Sisters and Bend, enjoy the views of the Sisters Mountains before heading up to the Mt. Bachelor ski resort. South of Mt. Bachelor is a relatively level upland area, rich in lakes and campsites. At nearly 100 miles, this is the longest section of the Trail.

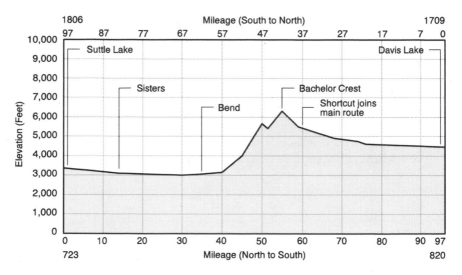

From Suttle Lake, head southeast on Highway 20/126. Eight miles down-hill from Suttle Lake is Indian Ford Campground (#1). Traffic can be heavy along this route. Six miles from Indian Ford Campground is the tourist-oriented city of Sisters with motels, grocery stores, and two campgrounds.

> *For backcountry enthusiasts there is a 29-mile, half-paved, half-dirt road "shortcut" between Sisters and Highway 46 west of Mt. Bachelor. Refer to the description of the shortcut later in this section. Highway 46 is part of the main route.*

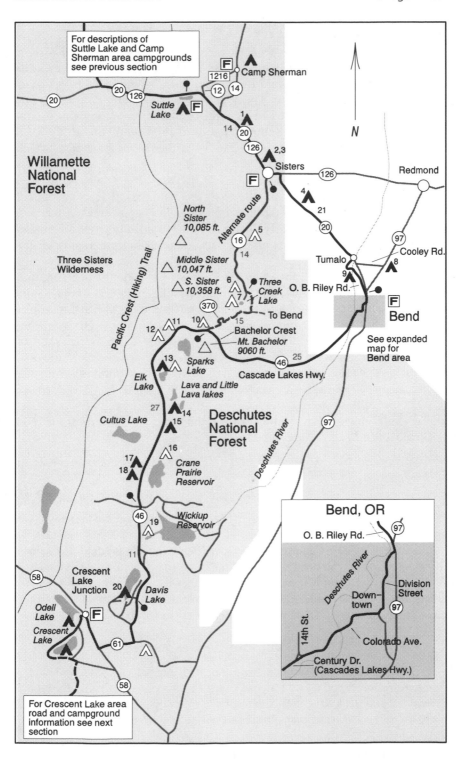

For descriptions of Suttle Lake and Camp Sherman area campgrounds see previous section

Camp Sherman

Suttle Lake

Sisters

Redmond

Willamette National Forest

Alternate route

North Sister 10,085 ft.

Three Sisters Wilderness

Middle Sister 10,047 ft.

S. Sister 10,358 ft.

Three Creek Lake

To Bend

Bachelor Crest

Mt. Bachelor 9060 ft.

Cascade Lakes Hwy.

Sparks Lake

Elk Lake

Lava and Little Lava lakes

Cultus Lake

Deschutes National Forest

Crane Prairie Reservoir

Wickiup Reservoir

Crescent Lake Junction

Odell Lake

Davis Lake

Crescent Lake

Tumalo

Cooley Rd.

O. B. Riley Rd.

Bend

See expanded map for Bend area

Deschutes River

For Crescent Lake area road and campground information see next section

**Bend, OR**

O. B. Riley Rd.

Deschutes River

Down-town

Division Street

Colorado Ave.

Century Dr. (Cascades Lakes Hwy.)

14th St.

## Continuing on the main route

The main route continues from Sisters on Highway 20/126 for a short distance. Where Highway 20 and Highway 126 separate, take Highway 20 as it departs to the southeast toward Bend. Four miles beyond Sisters is a KOA Kampground (#4) with a store. The countryside is virtually flat, with a few trees, some sagebrush, and nice views of the distant Sisters Mountains. About 10 miles from Sisters KOA Kampground, turn right onto O.B. Riley Road toward Tumalo State Park (#9). It is 2 miles farther to the state park, which allows camping.

Continue riding to the southeast as O.B. Riley Road goes uphill and connects with Highway 97 four miles past the state park. Bicycle about 0.2 mile on Highway 97 before turning right onto Division Street at the sign pointing to the exit for Bend City Center and Bachelor Butte. Follow Division Street through Bend, a tourist-oriented city large enough to supply all the amenities.

After approximately 2 miles on Division Street, and still in Bend, turn right onto Colorado Avenue, and cross the Deschutes River. About a mile later, veer left onto Century Drive (do not turn right onto 14th Street).

Eventually Century Drive becomes the Cascade Lakes Highway (Highway 46) and the upward climb begins through a forest. Five miles short of the highway's summit a deceptive downhill begins — it only lasts 2 miles and you still have 3 miles of uphill ahead. At the 6,300-foot summit is the popular Mt. Bachelor ski resort which is closed during the summer — Mt. Bachelor is a 9,000-foot flat-topped butte.

Two miles downhill on the other side of the summit is the turnoff for Todd Lake and Todd Lake Campground (#10).

*The shortcut from Sisters intersects Highway 46 and the main route here.*

Four miles past the turnoff to Todd Lake is Devil's Lake Campground (#12) at 5,500 feet. You are entering a beautiful cycling area with many lakes and campgrounds.

Past Devil's Lake Campground, you will encounter a gradual downslope for some miles as you head south, and there are many lava flows in the area. Forty-two miles from Mt. Bachelor crest you will reach the turnoff for the Davis Lake campgrounds of which East Davis Lake Campground (#20) is the most practical to use. There may be mosquitoes in the area.

## Sisters to Mt. Bachelor area shortcut

The dirt road portion of this shortcut is often sandy, rocky, and hard to get tire traction on, and a savings of time over the main route through Bend is doubtful. But the dirt portion is picturesque, rather wild, and closer to the Pacific Crest (Hiking) Trail, all of which would make the shortcut attractive to many. Considering that only 4-wheel drive motor vehicles can drive the dirt road, wide tires are recommended.

When I biked the unpaved road portion of the shortcut, in cool weather, with the sand compacted somewhat after a recent rain, and without full touring gear, the trip took three hours. In the heat of the summer and with 50 pounds of touring gear, the trip could take longer. Expect to walk your bike in some places.

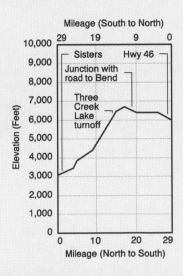

To take this shortcut route, in the city of Sisters follow the signs that point toward Three Creek Lake Campground (#7). The road (Forest Road 16) is paved and in excellent condition. Head south and climb gradually uphill — there is a 3,500-foot elevation gain overall — through semi-arid countryside. Seven miles from Sisters is Black Pine Spring Campground (#5). Six miles past the campground the road narrows and turns to gravel, and after another 2 miles you will reach a junction. To go to Three Creek Lake and its three campgrounds, turn right and bike a mile. The lake area is quite pretty and a store operates there during the summer months. Here the forest is fairly dense and in September 1988 the temperature dropped to 34 degrees overnight at this 6,300-foot elevation. There were also many deer and deer hunters in the area at the time.

From the junction near Three Creek Lake, head south on graveled Forest Road 370. There is considerable up and down work ahead. About 6 miles from the lake junction, shortly after crossing a stream and after a downhill stretch, you will reach a road junction. Turn right and continue on Forest Road 370 (a left turn will take you to the city of Bend). About 0.7 mile beyond the junction is spring water coming out of a pipe from the hillside and 0.2 mile beyond that a road goes off to the left. Do not take it; continue going straight as a small climb begins.

Two miles from the Bend turnoff and next to a stream is a nice, impromptu camping spot. There is more uphill after this, then some large, open, flat areas. You will get your first view of Mt. Bachelor in this area. Three miles after the previous impromptu campsite is another near a stream, with a table. Just beyond, a 3-mile downhill begins, ending at the turnoff for Todd Lake Campground (#10). One-half mile ahead is Highway 46 and the main route.

## Campgrounds

1. **Indian Ford Campground.** 5 miles northwest of Sisters on Highway 20. Has drinking water. Open 4/15–10/15. Forest Service.

2. **Sisters City Park Campground.** East end of Sisters on Highway 20/126. Has flush toilets. Municipal park.

3. **Circle Five Campground.** East end of Sisters on Highway 20/126. Has showers. Open all year. Privately run.

4. **Sisters KOA Kampground.** 4 miles southeast of Sisters on Highway 20. Has groceries, showers. Open all year. Privately run.

5. **Black Pine Spring Campground.** 8 miles south of Sisters on Highway 16. Has no drinking water. Open 5/15–10/15. Forest Service.

6. **Three Creek Meadow Campground.** Approximately 15 miles south of Sisters on Forest Road 16. Has no drinking water. Open 6/15–10/15. Forest Service.

7. **Driftwood and Three Creek Lake campgrounds.** Approximately 15 miles south of Sisters on Forest Road 16. Both are on Three Creek Lake and have no drinking water; a store is open during summer tourist months; has swimming. Open 6/15–10/15. Forest Service.

8. **Bend KOA Campground.** When biking southeast on Highway 20 toward Bend, after crossing the Deschutes River, turn left onto Cooley Road and continue several miles to the entrance. Alternately, when biking north from Bend, take Highway 97 three miles north. Has showers, pool, laundry, store. Open all year. Privately run.

9. **Tumalo State Park.** 5 miles northwest of Bend off Highway 20 on O.B. Riley Road. Has swimming. Open 4/15–10/31. State park.

10. **Todd Lake Campground.** 2 miles west of Mt. Bachelor crest on Highway 46, then 1 mile north on unpaved road. Has no drinking water. Forest Service.

11. **Soda Creek and Sparks Lake campgrounds.** 4 miles west of Mt. Bachelor crest on Highway 46. Sparks Lake Campground is 2 miles south on unpaved road. Both have no drinking water. Open 7/1–9/15. Forest Service.

12. **Devil's Lake Campground.** 7 miles southwest of Mt. Bachelor crest on Highway 46. Has no drinking water. Open 7/1–9/15. Forest Service.

13. **Elk Lake, Point, Beach, Sunset View, Little Fawn, Mallard Marsh, and South campgrounds.** All are near Elk Lake approximately 12 miles southwest of Mt. Bachelor crest on Highway 46. All have drinking water except Mallard Marsh and South campgrounds. All open 6/1–9/30. Forest Service.

14. **Little Lava Lake Campground.** 16 miles south of Mt. Bachelor crest on Highway 46. Has drinking water, swimming. Open 6/1–10/1. Forest Service.

15. **Deschutes Bridge Campground.** 19 miles south of Mt. Bachelor crest on Highway 46. Has drinking water. Open 6/1–10/1. Forest Service.

16. **Cow Meadow Campground.** 24 miles south of Mt. Bachelor crest on Highway 46, then 2 miles east on Forest Road 620. Has no drinking water. Open 5/1–10/15. Forest Service.

17. **Quinn River Campground.** On Crane Prairie Reservoir near Highway 46, 24 miles south of Mt. Bachelor crest. Has drinking water. Open 7/1–9/30. Forest Service.

18. **Rock Creek Campground.** On Crane Prairie Reservoir near Highway 46, 27 miles south of Mt. Bachelor crest. Has drinking water. Open 5/1–9/30. Forest Service.

19. **North Davis Creek Campground.** On an arm of Wickiup Reservoir near Highway 46, 34 miles south of Mt. Bachelor crest. Has no drinking water. Open 5/1–10/31. Forest Service.

20. **East Davis Lake Campground.** Turn off Highway 46 forty-two miles south of Mt. Bachelor crest, bike a short distance, turn left onto a gravel road, bike 0.5 mile, then turn right and bike 0.5 mile to campsite on south end of Davis Lake. Has drinking water. Open 5/1–10/31. Two other campgrounds, Lava Flow and West Davis Lake, are also on Davis Lake but are much further from the highway. Lava Flow Campground does not have drinking water. Open 5/15–10/31. Forest Service.

# Davis Lake
# to
# Diamond Lake

51 miles  •  A Seldom-Used Road

Half of this mostly-forested section is unpaved. From Davis Lake, the Trail rises to Crescent Lake Junction and Crescent Lake on a paved road, then switches to a dirt road for the journey over 5,850-foot Windigo Pass. The final 5 miles to popular Diamond Lake are paved.

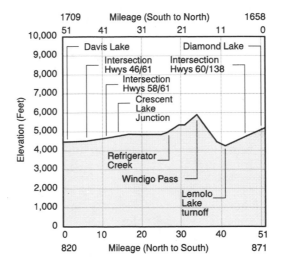

Continue south from the Davis Lake area on Highway 46 for 7 miles, then turn right onto Highway 61 and bike gradually uphill for 3 miles before reaching busy Highway 58. Turn right onto Highway 58 and bicycle another 3 miles gradually uphill to Crescent Lake Junction. The town, the last food stop before Diamond Lake, has a general store with groceries and a post office.

From Crescent Lake Junction, take Forest Road 60 southwest (a left turn). After 2 miles and several bends in the road, turn right, continuing on paved Forest Road 60 to the southwest. A short distance beyond, on Crescent Lake, is Crescent Lake Campground (#2). Follow Forest Road 60 around the west side of the lake. About 5 miles from Crescent Lake Campground the pavement turns to hard-packed dirt. Just beyond is Spring Campground (#3) on Crescent Lake. Four miles from that campground turn hard right and remain on Forest Road 60, again heading southwest. A sign at this turn confirms that you are heading toward Windigo Pass and Highway 138.

This road is also unpaved and portions are sandy. Your bike may want to

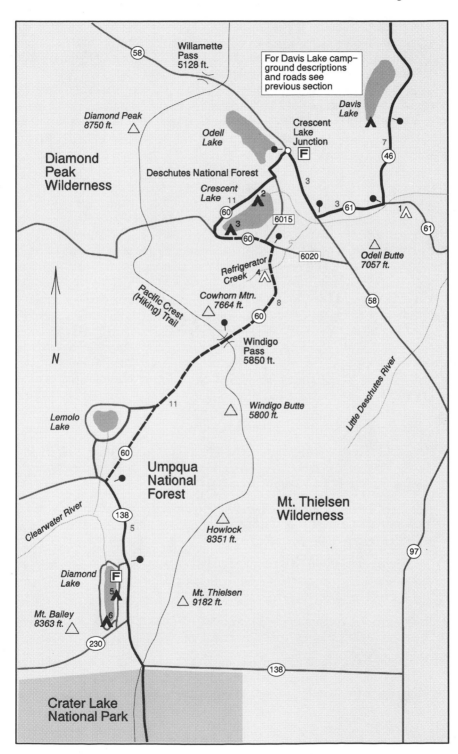

For Davis Lake camp-
ground descriptions
and roads see
previous section

Willamette
Pass
5128 ft.

58

Davis
Lake

Diamond Peak
8750 ft.

Diamond
Peak
Wilderness

Odell
Lake

Crescent
Lake
Junction

F

7

46

Deschutes National Forest

3

Crescent
Lake    11

60

2

3

6015

60

61

3

61

1

6020

Odell Butte
7057 ft.

Refrigerator
Creek

4

5

Cowhorn Mtn.
7664 ft.

8

Pacific Crest
(Hiking) Trail

60

58

N

Windigo
Pass
5850 ft.

Little Deschutes River

11

Windigo Butte
5800 ft.

Lemolo
Lake

60

Umpqua
National
Forest

Mt. Thielsen
Wilderness

Clearwater River

138

5

Howlock
8351 ft.

97

Diamond
Lake

F

5

Mt. Thielsen
9182 ft.

Mt. Bailey
8363 ft.

6

230

138

Crater Lake
National Park

slip and slide, so stay in low gear, try to ride on tire tracks, and keep your shoes out of your toe clips if you use them. Two miles from the previous hard right turn, shortly after crossing over Refrigerator Creek, keep to the right at a "Y" in the road and continue uphill toward Windigo Pass.

One June when my friend and I rode this section, we ran into snow on the north side of the pass and had difficulty pushing our laden bikes over more than a mile of it, even though it was hard-packed. On the downhill on the other side of the pass, a small melted-snow lake blocked the road. We had to push our bikes through it.

Seven miles from the "Y", 5,850-foot Windigo Pass is reached. This area, a crossing point for the Pacific Crest (Hiking) Trail, is remote with dense forest and very few cars.

Continue downhill on the unpaved road. Seven miles from the crest you will have the choice of continuing gently uphill on straight, unpaved Forest Road 60 for 4 miles to Highway 138 or making a right turn toward Lemolo Lake onto a paved road system that will also take you to Highway 138, but is 3 miles longer. If using the paved road, follow it for 2 miles before turning left at a "Y" near the lake. Bike about 2 miles before making another left turn and biking about 2 miles to a left turn onto Highway 138.

Whichever route you take, you will be turning left onto Highway 138 and heading south. The turnoff to Diamond Lake is about 5 miles away and it is a mile to the lake. At the lake there is a store, lodge, dining room, and post office. Diamond Lake Campground (#5) is two miles further south on the road next to the lake. I found mosquitoes here one August.

## Campgrounds

1. **Crescent Creek Campground.** On Highway 61, 0.5 mile east of the intersection of Highway 46 and Highway 61. Has no drinking water; is very small. Open 5/1–10/31. Forest Service.

2. **Crescent Lake Campground.** 3 miles southwest of Crescent Lake Junction on Forest Road 60. Has drinking water, swimming, groceries (available in Crescent Lake Junction). Open 5/15–9/30. Forest Service.

3. **Spring Campground.** At Crescent Lake, 8 miles southwest of Crescent Lake Junction on Forest Road 60. Has drinking water, swimming. Open 6/1– 9/30. Forest Service.

4. **Impromptu Campground.** Where Refrigerator Creek crosses Forest Road 60 about 13 miles from Crescent Lake Junction.

5. **Diamond Lake Campground.** From Highway 138 take signed turnoff for 2 miles to visitor center, restaurant, store, lodge and post office. Campground is 1 mile south of visitor center on road next to lake. Has drinking water, swimming. Open 6/1–10/15. Forest Service.

6. **Broken Arrow Campground.** On south end of Diamond Lake, 2 miles south of campground #5 on same road. Has drinking water, nearby store, pizza place. Open 5/21–9/15. Forest Service.

Snow on the north side of Windigo Pass slowed progress during a June trip.

# Diamond Lake
# to
# Willow Lake

86 miles • The Trail's High Point in Oregon

This is another long section. After Diamond Lake, you will climb 2,500 feet to 5-mile-wide Crater Lake, located at the top of a high, collapsed volcano. After following Crater Lake rim for 6 miles, the Trail drops 5,000 feet over 33 miles to the town of Prospect. After crossing several rivers and a ridge, this section ends at Willow Lake. If you intend to go all the way to Willow Lake, do not stay too long at Crater Lake.

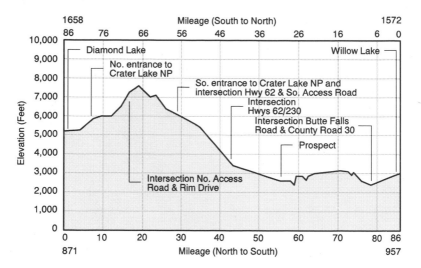

From the Diamond Lake turnoff on Highway 138, bike south on Highway 138 for 7 miles, then turn right onto the North Access Road and head into Crater Lake National Park. You will soon pass the north entrance station which is not always manned.

*Except in very heavy snow years, the north entrance into Crater Lake is open from about June 15 to mid-September or the first heavy snow. You may wish to check with park headquarters if you are travelling early or late in the season. If the road to Crater Lake is closed, the low elevation road (Highway 230) running to the west of the park will connect you with the rest of the Trail (see map for details).*

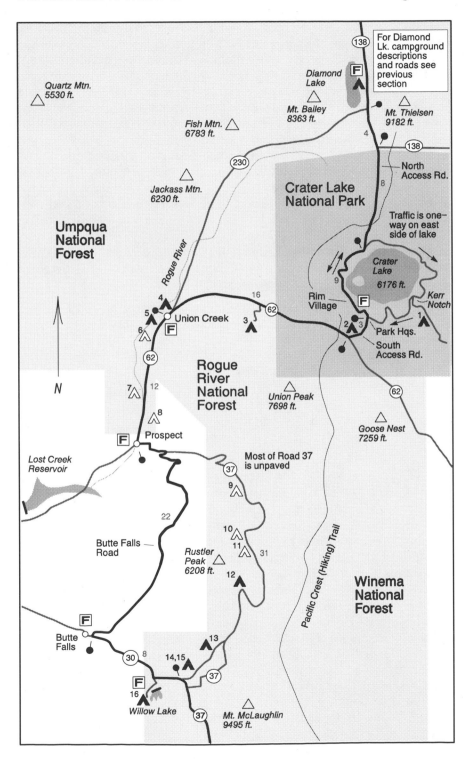

For Diamond Lk. campground descriptions and roads see previous section

Diamond Lake

Quartz Mtn. 5530 ft.

Mt. Bailey 8363 ft.

Mt. Thielsen 9182 ft.

Fish Mtn. 6783 ft.

North Access Rd.

Crater Lake National Park

Jackass Mtn. 6230 ft.

Rogue River

Umpqua National Forest

Traffic is one-way on east side of lake

Crater Lake 6176 ft.

Kerr Notch

Rim Village

Union Creek

Park Hqs.

Rogue River National Forest

South Access Rd.

N

Union Peak 7698 ft.

Goose Nest 7259 ft.

Prospect

Lost Creek Reservoir

Most of Road 37 is unpaved

Butte Falls Road

Rustler Peak 6208 ft.

Pacific Crest (Hiking) Trail

Winema National Forest

Butte Falls

Willow Lake

Mt. McLaughlin 9495 ft.

Soon after the north entrance station, the road passes through a flat, desert-like area. Here, the pumice and ash from ancient volcanic eruptions is so deep (50 feet or so) that virtually nothing grows. The Pacific Crest (Hiking) Trail crosses the road here. Then it is up, up, up, past small clumps of trees until 7 miles from the entrance station you get your first view of Crater Lake from Rim Drive. Do not be surprised to find deep snow along the roads near and around Crater Lake — an average of 50 feet of snow falls at the top each winter and some usually remains into the summer.

The crater, or caldera, was created when an ancient 12,000-foot volcano collapsed. Rain and snow melt filled the caldera and created the lake, which is 6 miles long, 4 miles wide, and 1,932 feet deep, making it the deepest lake in the United States. The elevation of the lake surface is about 6,200 feet. Rising out of the water on the west end of the lake is a mysterious-looking cinder cone called Wizard Island.

Turn right onto Rim Drive. The air will be cool on the 7,000-foot highway. Rim Village is a welcome sight 6 miles away, with a cafeteria, small grocery store, and lodge. Watch out for sightseeing drivers.

### Rim Drive – East Side

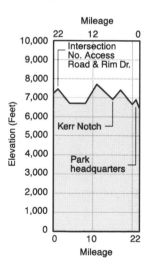

*The entire rim drive around the lake measures 33 miles and usually opens in mid-July (refer to the elevation profile for Rim Drive on east side of Crater Lake). Cyclists can turn left onto Rim Drive and bike 4 miles to Cleetwood Trail, which is the only trail down to water's edge. After that point, Rim Drive becomes a one-way road heading south on the east side of Crater Lake.*

Heading south again on the west rim from Rim Village, ride 3 miles before turning right onto the South Access Road in the direction of Medford and Klamath Falls. At this junction is the park headquarters and the end of the east rim road. In this area you will begin one of the longer downhills of the Trail. On the way down, about 3 miles from Rim Drive, is Mazama Campground (#2) and the Annie Spring Entrance Station.

At Highway 62, turn right toward Medford. Fifteen miles downhill is the intersection with Highway 230. Continue on Highway 62. Nearby, the wild and woolly Rogue River parallels the highway in a gorge.

One mile south of the Highway 230 intersection, the town of Union Creek has a campground, store, and cafe. Twelve miles later, after a seemingly endless downhill, the town of Prospect marks the bottom of the "hill." Turn left onto 1st Street and go into town. You will find a large grocery store and post office. Take Butte Falls Road (which has little traffic) east out of town.

Wizard Island in Crater Lake.

Here the geology changes from heavy doses of pumice to seemingly pure sand.

In the first 7 miles from Prospect you cross both the middle and south forks of the Rogue River and gain elevation. Several miles later a plateau begins which continues for about 11 miles before a downgrade is reached. The landscape varies from lush woods to cut-back areas.

After a 4-mile downhill, you reach the intersection of Butte Falls Road and County Road 30. The town of Butte Falls, which has a grocery store, cafe, and snack bar, but no motel, lies 0.6 mile to the right. However, to follow the main route, turn left onto County Road 30. There is no campground near this junction, although there is a fish hatchery where you can ask for fresh, cool water. From this point ride gradually uphill for 7 miles to the turnoff for Willow Lake Campground (#16). The campground is 2 miles off the highway and has a store and restaurant. If you have bicycled all the way from Diamond Lake with full touring gear you will be hungry and tired.

Several miles beyond the Willow Lake turnoff is Whiskey Springs Campground (#14) and Fourbit Ford Campground (#15).

### Campgrounds

1. **Lost Creek Campground.** In the Kerr Notch area on the southeast side of Crater Lake, 3 miles off Rim Drive and 700 feet below. Primitive; no fee. Has flush toilets. Usually open by mid-July. National Park Service.

2. **Mazama Campground.** 3 miles southwest of Crater Lake National Park Headquarters at junction of South Access Road and Highway 62. Has drinking water. Open 6/15–9/26. National Park Service.

3. **Huckleberry City Campground.** Turn off Highway 62 about 2 miles west of Crater Lake National Park boundary, then travel 4 miles south on Forest Road 60 with a climb of 1,000 feet. No fee. Has drinking water. Open 7/1–10/19. Forest Service.

4. **Farewell Bend Campground.** 12 miles north of Prospect on Highway 62. Has drinking water. Open 5/23–9/10. Forest Service.

5. **Union Creek Campground.** 11 miles north of Prospect on Highway 62. Has drinking water. Open 5/23–9/10. Forest Service.

6. **Natural Bridge Campground.** 10 miles north of Prospect on Highway 62, then 1 mile west on Forest Road 300. Has no drinking water; no fee. Open 5/23–9/10. Forest Service.

7. **River Bridge Campground.** 4 miles north of Prospect, then 1 mile off Highway 62. Has no drinking water. Open 5/23–9/30. Forest Service.

8. **Mill Creek Campground.** 2 miles north of Prospect, then 1 mile northeast on Road 030. Has no drinking water. Open 5/23–9/30. Forest Service.

9. **Imnaha Campground.** 11 miles southeast of Prospect on Highway 37. Has no drinking water. Forest Service.

10. **South Fork Campground.** 16 miles southeast of Prospect on Highway 37. Has no drinking water. Forest Service.

11. **Big Ben Campground.** 17 miles southeast of Prospect on Highway 37. Has no drinking water. Forest Service.

12. **Parker Meadows Campground.** On Highway 37, 11 miles northeast of the intersection of Highway 30 and Highway 37. Has drinking water. Open 6/15–9/30. Forest Service.

13. **Snowshoe Campground.** 7 miles northeast of the intersection of Highway 30 and Highway 37, then about 1 mile off Highway 37. Has drinking water. Open 5/22–10/31. Forest Service.

14. **Whiskey Springs Campground.** 10 miles southeast of Butte Falls just off County Road 30 on Road 3065. Has drinking water. Open 5/24–9/10. Forest Service.

15. **Fourbit Ford Campground.** On Road 3065, a short distance beyond campground #14. Has drinking water. Open 5/22–10/31. Forest Service.

16. **Willow Lake Campground.** 7 miles southeast of Butte Falls on County Road 30, then 2 miles south on paved road. Has store, restaurant, showers, swimming. Open 4/15–10/15. County.

# Willow Lake
# to
# Ashland

<u>44 miles • Beautiful Forests</u>

"Water, woods and volcanoes" could describe much of this area — in fact much of the Cascades. After a short uphill, the Trail levels out in a beautiful forest. The ride down to Ashland at the end of this section is serpentine and steep.

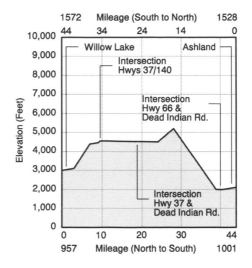

From the turnoff to Willow Lake, proceed east for 2 miles on County Road 30 (passing the turnoff to Whiskey Springs Campground) before the road makes a right turn to the south, becomes Highway 37, and begins angling upward.

About 9 miles from the Whiskey Springs Campground turnoff you will intersect Highway 140. This area has some magnificent forests. Now, despite what some maps show, make a right turn onto Highway 140, bike a few yards, then turn left and continue south on Highway 37. Shortly you will reach North Fork Campground (#2).

In my opinion this is one of the lovelier roads of the entire Pacific Crest Bicycle Trail. It has little traffic, is usually cool, has a good road surface, and passes through a beautiful forest with several ancient lava flows.

Six miles from Highway 140 is Daley Creek Campground (#4), followed 2 miles later by the intersection with Dead Indian Road; turn right here. The landscape now becomes rather dry, open and flat. After 5 miles on Dead Indian Road, a long uphill pull begins that crests 4 miles later at 5,200 feet.

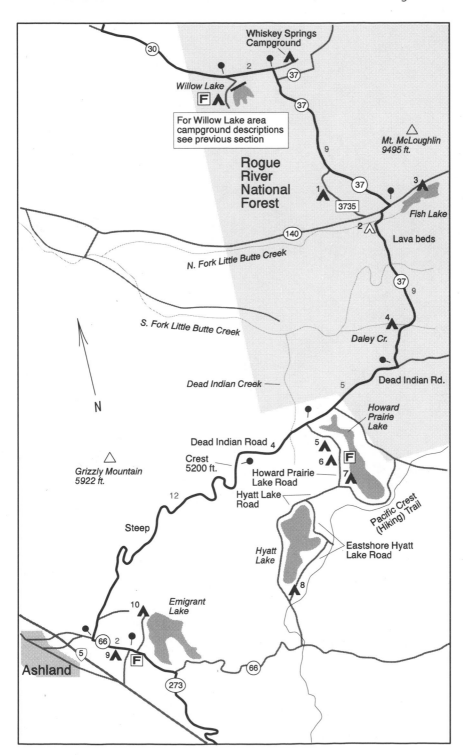

Whiskey Springs
Campground

30

2

37

Willow Lake

F

For Willow Lake area
campground descriptions
see previous section

9

Mt. McLoughlin
9495 ft.

Rogue
River
National
Forest

1

37

3

3735

Fish Lake

140

2

Lava beds

37

9

N. Fork Little Butte Creek

S. Fork Little Butte Creek

4

Daley Cr.

Dead Indian Creek

5

Dead Indian Rd.

N

Howard
Prairie
Lake

Dead Indian Road  4

Crest
5200 ft.

5

6

F

Grizzly Mountain
5922 ft.

Howard Prairie
Lake Road

7

Hyatt Lake
Road

12

Pacific Crest
(Hiking) Trail

Steep

Hyatt
Lake

Eastshore Hyatt
Lake Road

8

10

Emigrant
Lake

66

2

9

F

5

Ashland

66

273

Dead Indian Road near Ashland.

You will now see the deep valley, surrounded by picturesque mountains, where Ashland and Freeway 5 are located. Before beginning the long, steep, and very curvey downhill to Ashland, check your brakes. It is also advisable to stop somewhere on the way down to let your rims cool. Depending on the amount of weight you are carrying and how fast you go, your rims may heat up too much from braking and cause a flat.

Twelve miles from the crest, after Dead Indian Road has leveled off, turn left onto Highway 66 (do not make a premature left turn toward Emigrant Reservoir). Glenyan KOA Kampground (#9) is 2 miles ahead.

Refer to the map if you wish to go into Ashland, with its many motels, restaurants, and Shakespearean theater. There is also at least one bicycle repair shop in Ashland.

The last time I bicycled this valley the temperature exceeded 100 degrees. Fortunately, my partner and I were able to sit in a cool creek adjacent to our campsite.

### Campgrounds

1. **Willow Prairie Campground.** Leave Highway 37 about 7 miles southeast of the Willow Lake turnoff, then 1 mile on Forest Road 3735. Has drinking water. Open 5/22–10/31. Forest Service.

2. **North Fork Campground.** Just off Highway 140 on Highway 37. Has no drinking water, but stream water can be purified. Open 5/28–9/6. Forest Service.

3. **Doe Point and Fish Lake campgrounds.** On Highway 140 at Fish Lake, 2 miles east of the intersection of Highway 37 and Highway 140. Has drinking water. Open 7/1–10/31. Forest Service.

4. **Daley Creek and Beaver Dam campgrounds.** On Highway 37, 2 miles north of the intersection of Highway 37 and Dead Indian Road. Both have drinking water. Open 5/28–9/6. Forest Service.

5. **Grizzly Creek Campground.** On Howard Prairie Lake, 2 miles south of Dead Indian Road on Howard Prairie Lake Road. Has drinking water. Open 4/15–10/15. County campground.

6. **Howard Prairie Lake Resort.** On Howard Prairie Lake, 3 miles south of Dead Indian Road on Howard Prairie Lake Road. Has laundry, groceries, restaurant, swimming. Open 4/15-10/31. Privately run.

7. **Willow Point Campground.** On Howard Prairie Lake, 4 miles south of Dead Indian Road on Howard Prairie Lake Road, then 0.4 mile east on unnamed road along Willow Creek. Has drinking water. Open 4/15–10/15. County.

8. **Hyatt Lake Campground.** About 4 miles south of Dead Indian Road on Howard Prairie Lake Road, then 1 mile southwest on Eastshore Hyatt Lake Road, then 3 miles south on Eastshore Hyatt Lake Road. Located on south end of Hyatt Lake. Flush toilets and showers. Opens about April 15. Bureau of Land Management.

9. **Glenyan KOA Kampground.** On Highway 66 near Ashland, 2 miles southeast of the intersection of Dead Indian Road and Highway 66. Has laundry, groceries, pool. Open 2/20-10/31. Privately run.

10. **Emigrant Lake Campground.** Turnoff is 3 miles southeast of the intersection of Dead Indian Road and Highway 66. Bike 1 mile to campsites near Emigrant Lake Reservoir. Has drinking water, nearby store. County.

# Region 3
# Northern California

Mt. Shasta looms behind a frisky colt near Weed.

# Ashland, OR
# to
# Hamburg

*Includes a paved shortcut from
Siskiyou Pass in Oregon to Gazelle in California.*

66 miles • Following a High, Isolated Ridgeline

This section, after an initial 4,800-foot climb on a paved road, contains the longest unpaved stretch of road (40 miles) on the Trail. Fortunately, the unpaved road is hard-packed and not difficult to ride, but rains can change that.

The unpaved main route follows the Pacific Crest (Hiking) Trail closely along a high ridge. Those of you who enjoy backcountry riding will find this road very rewarding with its forests, deer, and excellent vistas into the mountains of Oregon and California.

On the main route between Siskiyou Pass and Horse Creek there are no stores or guaranteed sources of water, so bring plenty of food and water in addition to some sort of water purification tablets or device. Also, be prepared for breezy, cool-to-cold weather at these higher altitudes.

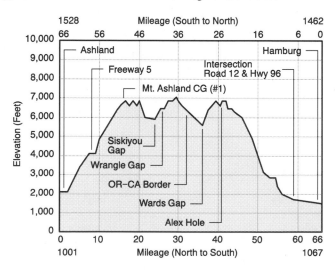

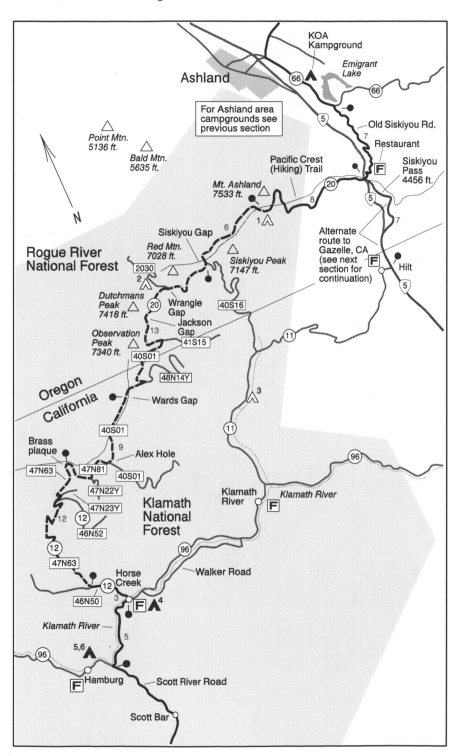

KOA
Kampground

Emigrant
Lake

Ashland

66

66

For Ashland area
campgrounds see
previous section

5

Old Siskiyou Rd.

7

Restaurant

Point Mtn.
5136 ft.

Siskiyou
Pass
4456 ft.

Bald Mtn.
5635 ft.

Pacific Crest
(Hiking) Trail

F

Mt. Ashland
7533 ft.

20

8

5

N

Siskiyou Gap

6

1

7

Rogue River
National Forest

Red Mtn.
7028 ft.

Siskiyou Peak
7147 ft.

Alternate
route to
Gazelle, CA
(see next
section for
continuation)

F

Hilt

2030

5

2

Dutchmans
Peak
7418 ft.

20

Wrangle
Gap

40S16

Observation
Peak
7340 ft.

13

Jackson
Gap

11

40S01

41S15

48N14Y

3

Oregon

California

Wards Gap

11

40S01

Brass
plaque

9

Alex Hole

96

47N63

47N81

40S01

47N22Y

Klamath
River

Klamath River

47N23Y

Klamath
National
Forest

F

12

12

46N52

12

96

47N63

Horse
Creek

Walker Road

12

46N50

3

F

4

Klamath River

5

96

5,6

Hamburg

F

Scott River Road

Scott Bar

Trading stories at Siskiyou Pass.

From the KOA campground near Ashland, continue south on Highway 66 for 2 miles, then turn right onto Old Siskiyou Road. By using this road you avoid the freeway over Siskiyou Pass.

After a mile on Old Siskiyou Road, a 5-mile winding climb begins, passing through woods and by scattered homes, until the road levels off at a res-

taurant. Pass under Freeway 5 and make a left turn at the T-intersection. The
Pacific Crest (Hiking) Trail crosses the road nearby.

*At this point you can follow the easier, paved shortcut to Gazelle,
roughly paralleling the freeway (refer to the description of the shortcut
later in this section), or you can take the challenging, partly-unpaved
main route, which is 94 miles and at least one day longer. The main
route runs close to the Pacific Crest (Hiking) Trail and is more
picturesque and quiet.*

### Continuing on the main route

After making the left turn at the T-intersection at the end of Old Siskiyou
Road, ride a short distance and turn right at a sign which reads "Colestin
Road–Mt. Ashland Ski Area–Mt. Ashland Road." Begin climbing on new,
excellent, paved Forest Road 20 through nicely-forested areas. Seven miles
from the sign you will reach the Mt. Ashland ski resort.

Head west through the parking lot past the ski resort (closed in summer),
and continue on a hard-packed gravel and dirt road, which is still signed as
Forest Road 20. One mile beyond the parking lot is Mt. Ashland Campground
(#1), but water is not available there year around. Nearby to the north is
7,533-foot Mt. Ashland. Just past the campground, stay left on Forest Road
20 as you pass a road on your right. This area is very alpine and isolated, and
there are beautiful vistas into the mountains to the north. The wind is usually
active because of the high elevation (6,000–7,000 feet).

About 2 miles from the campground, pass Forest Road 40S30 on your left
and continue on Forest Road 20. Three miles later is Meridian Overlook, and
after another 3 miles you will reach Siskiyou Gap.

*In an emergency situation, unpaved Forest Road 40S16, which departs
Forest Road 20 to the left at Siskiyou Gap, can be used to get to
civilization on an all-downhill route. Follow it for 12 miles (past many
intersections with other roads) to the intersection with Forest Road 11
(also called 48N01). Turn right onto mostly-unpaved Forest Road 11 and
in 5 miles you will reach Beaver Creek Campground (#3). After 9 miles
on Forest Road 11, turn right onto Highway 96 and bike 0.5 mile into
the little town of Klamath River which has a store, phone, and post office.*

Continuing on Forest Road 20 from Siskiyou Gap, it is 3 miles to Wrangle
Gap and a crossing of the Pacific Crest (Hiking) Trail. A sign points to
Wrangle Camp (#2) which is 0.5 mile to the right and down an incline. The
camp is in a beautifully-forested area and has a large, well-built, wooden
shelter. When I visited one July, the hand pump was not producing any water
and there were no campers.

Three miles beyond Wrangle Gap and in the vicinity of Jackson Gap is an
open area that is the 7,000-foot high point of this section of the Trail. There

can be spots of snow at this elevation well into the summer as well as cattle
with cowbells. After this point, continue as Forest Road 20 becomes Forest
Road 40S01. About 2 miles from the crest is a T-intersection. Make a hard
right here and remain on Forest Road 40S01 — a left turn will put you on
Forest Road 41S15.

A mile from the T-intersection are a few buildings, followed by a spring
or small stream, and just beyond is the California border. Now the road seems
less used, with weeds in its center, as it heads downhill towards Wards Gap.
Pass the intersections with Forest Roads 48N16 and 48N14Y, make a hard
right turn after 48N14Y, and continue on Forest Road 40S01. Some logging
has been done in this area. Three miles from the border, at Wards Gap, is a
spot where many roads intersect.

Continue on Forest Road 40S01, heading uphill through a rich forest with
ferns. Three miles from Wards Gap is a stark, open area, and 5 miles away is
the intersection of Forest Road 40S01 and Forest Road 47N81 at a place
called Alex Hole. Forest Road 40S01 would take you all the way down to
Highway 96 and the Klamath River. Instead, make a hard right turn onto
Forest Road 47N81 and shortly you will be treated to some beautiful vistas.

Three miles from the intersection of Forest Road 47N81 and Forest Road
40S01, 47N81 takes a hard left at a brass plaque marking the death of a hiker,
Max Paul (no relation, thank you), and becomes Forest Road 47N63. Now
begins the section's 15-mile, 5,000-foot downhill ride.

As you descend keep your speed low because there are occasional ruts in
the road. About 2 miles downhill from the plaque, make a hard right turn and
continue downhill on Forest Road 47N63 instead of making a left turn onto
Forest Road 47N23Y. Be aware that there are no signs at this intersection.
Refer to the map.

Some clear-cut logging along this stretch of road makes the area less than
beautiful.

Soon Forest Road 47N63 is also signed as Forest Road 12. Follow this
road downhill, being careful to avoid rocks in the roadway, and 12 miles from
the brass plaque make a left turn onto paved Forest Road 46N50. Continue
to ride slightly downhill for 2 miles until you reach Highway 96 and the
Klamath River. Highway 96 is a somewhat narrow, busy highway with many
logging trucks and much tourist traffic. Be careful!

A left turn onto Highway 96 and a short ride will take you to the Horse
Creek store and post office. However, to continue on the main route, turn
right onto Highway 96 and ride 5 miles to the intersection with Scott River
Road. If you wish to continue on the main route, turn left here. If you wish
to use the nearby campgrounds or store, remain on Highway 96 and ride
several miles to their location near the little town of Hamburg. Hamburg's
Rainbow Resort sells groceries year around.

## Siskiyou Pass to Gazelle shortcut

*This shortcut begins on the map in this section and continues on the map in the next section.*

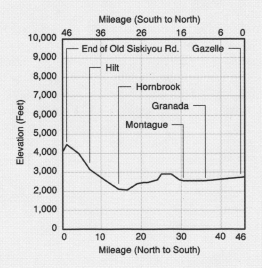

After passing under Freeway 5 and making a left turn at the T-intersection at the end of Old Siskiyou Road, continue south on the blacktop road.

*If the blacktop road is blocked you will need to take Freeway 5 by turning right after you pass under the freeway (the freeway is legal to ride in this instance because it would be the only road available for use when heading south). If you use the freeway, be sure that you ride as far as possible to the right. The 6-mile descent can be cold, and just over the border into California the town of Hilt has a restaurant and small store.*

If the not-too-well-maintained blacktop road is open, continue south on it and pass under Freeway 5 a second time. After 2 miles you will reach 4,456-foot Siskiyou Pass. The wind can be strong here, but weather permitting, the overlook provides good views into California.

After 2 miles of downhill from the pass, turn right at a "Y" in the road. Two miles later, the road joins Freeway 5. Coast down the freeway for 2 miles, and just after crossing into California you will reach the exit for Hilt. You will find a service station, restaurant, and small store here.

From Hilt, continue 6 miles down Freeway 5 and take the Hornbrook exit off the freeway. In 1 mile you will reach Hornbrook with several grocery stores and a semi-hippie atmosphere. Ride straight through town, then a short distance beyond turn left onto Copco Road, and ride along the Klamath River for 2 miles. Turn right onto Ager Road, cross the river, and head south toward Montague 14 miles away. On Ager Road you will be negotiating small hills in an easy upward climb for 8 miles before beginning a long, gentle downhill into Montague, which has a store and several restaurants. Mt. Shasta usually dominates the skyline here — it's 40 miles to the south.

In Montague, continue generally straight through town and follow Montague-Grenada Road south about 6 miles to the tiny town of Grenada which has a convenience store. In Granada, turn right and bike a short distance over the freeway, then immediately turn left onto the paved freeway frontage road (Old 99 Highway). The town of Gazelle is 9 miles to the south on this level route. Gazelle has a small store in a filling station.

The only campground near the alternate route between Siskiyou Pass and Gazelle is Tree of Heaven Campground, 7 miles west of Freeway 5 on Highway 96. Refer to Section 3-2 for details.

*In Gazelle you rejoin the main route which continues in Section 3-2.*

## Campgrounds

1. **Mt. Ashland Campground.** On Forest Road 20, 1 mile west of Mt. Ashland Ski Resort parking lot. Drinking water may not be available. Forest Service.

2. **Wrangle Campground.** 10 miles west of Mt. Ashland Ski Resort on Forest Road 20, then 0.5 mile north on Forest Road 2030. Has a shelter; drinking water may not be available. Open 6/10–10/28. Forest Service.

3. **Beaver Creek Campground.** On Forest Road 11 about 6 miles south of the intersection of Forest Road 40S16 and Forest Road 11, or about 4 miles north of the intersection of Forest Road 11 and Highway 96. Has no drinking water, but stream water can be purified. Open 6/1–10/31. Forest Service.

4. **Big Foot Recreational Resort.** On Walker Road, 10 miles west of town of Klamath River and 1 mile east of town of Horse Creek. Has showers, swimming; groceries available at Horse Creek. Open 4/1–10/31. Privately run.

5. **Sarah Totten Campground.** On Highway 96 about 2 miles west of the intersection of Highway 96 and Scott River Road at the little town of Hamburg. Has drinking water; groceries available at nearby Rainbow Resort. Open all year. Forest Service.

6. **Steelhead Lodge and RV Park.** Adjacent to campground #5. Has showers, swimming, laundromat, small restaurant. Open all year. Privately run.

A morning fog drifts over Road 20 in the Siskiyou Mountains.

# Hamburg
# to
# Weed

### 92 miles • Gold Mining Country

Using all paved roads, this long section follows the Scott River for much of its length. Begin with a 20-mile ride up a richly-forested valley before entering flat farming land. After Callahan, the day's work begins — a 2,000-foot climb over Gazelle Mountain Summit. This section ends in the thriving city of Weed along Freeway 5.

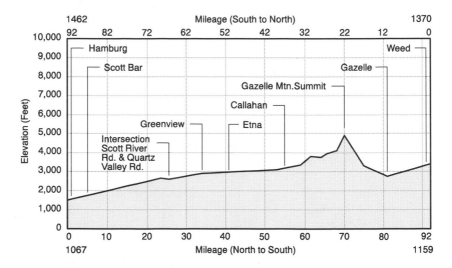

From Highway 96 near Hamburg, head south on Scott River Road up a beautiful valley, hemmed in by lushly-forested mountains. After 3 miles is the small town of Scott Bar, which has no stores. It is the site of the first gold strike in Siskiyou County.

Past Scott Bar the road becomes narrow and curvy — watch out for oncoming cars. There are a few scattered homes in the valley. Ten miles from Scott Bar is Bridge Flat Campground (#1); Spring Flat Campground (#2) and Indian Scotty Campground (#3) follow in short order.

After gaining more elevation, and 5 miles beyond Indian Scotty Campground, the road emerges from the canyon into flat meadow and farm land with some clusters of homes. Seven miles from Indian Scotty Campground turn right onto Quartz Valley Road at a little red schoolhouse which is now a home. Cross a large, then a small bridge (do not take Dangel Road or East

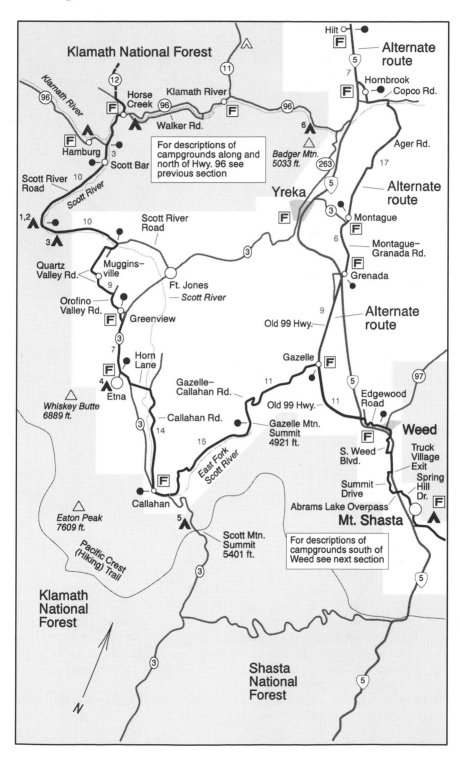

Klamath National Forest

Klamath River

Horse Creek

Klamath River

Walker Rd.

Hamburg

Scott Bar

Scott River Road

Scott River

For descriptions of campgrounds along and north of Hwy. 96 see previous section

Badger Mtn. 5033 ft.

Hilt

Hornbrook

Copco Rd.

Ager Rd.

Alternate route

Yreka

Montague

Montague-Granada Rd.

Alternate route

Scott River Road

Mugginsville

Ft. Jones

Scott River

Quartz Valley Rd.

Orofino Valley Rd.

Greenview

Grenada

Horn Lane

Gazelle-Callahan Rd.

Old 99 Hwy.

Alternate route

Gazelle

Etna

Whiskey Butte 6889 ft.

Callahan Rd.

Old 99 Hwy.

Gazelle Mtn. Summit 4921 ft.

Edgewood Road

Weed

Truck Village Exit

S. Weed Blvd.

Spring Hill Dr.

Summit Drive

Abrams Lake Overpass

Mt. Shasta

Callahan

Eaton Peak 7609 ft.

Pacific Crest (Hiking) Trail

Scott Mtn. Summit 5401 ft.

For descriptions of campgrounds south of Weed see next section

Klamath National Forest

Shasta National Forest

N

Downtown Etna.

Quartz Road), and head briefly west through irrigated land before turning south and continuing on Quartz Valley Road. Four miles from the intersection of Scott River Road and Quartz Valley Road, follow Quartz Valley Road as it turns left and heads east. Shortly, you will pass through Mugginsville, a quaint little town with no stores.

Continue on Quartz Valley Road another 2 miles before reaching the intersection with Orofino Valley Road. Turn right onto Orofino Valley Road and bike a little over a mile into the town of Greenview, one of the more interesting little towns around. It has a store.

In Greenview, turn right onto Main Street and travel about 0.5 mile beyond the town to Highway 3. Turn right onto Highway 3 and continue south on the nice paved shoulder for about 7 miles to the turnoff for the town of Etna. Towns in this area are interesting — I recommend departing Highway 3 to take a look at downtown Etna, which speaks of the 30s or 40s. Like Scott Bar, this town has strong connections to gold rush days. Etna has plenty of stores and at least one restaurant. Don't be surprised to see an elephant in a field behind Dotty's Restaurant at the turnoff to Etna.

From the turnoff to Etna, continue southeast on Highway 3 and travel a short distance — just past the bridge over Etna Creek — before turning left onto Horn Lane and biking a mile to a T-intersection. Turn right here and head south on East Callahan Road, which later becomes Callahan Road, and follow the California-Oregon stagecoach route of 1851-1886. This area has some irrigated farming, and huge black piles of gold mining tailings are seen along Scott River.

Ten miles from the T-intersection, Callahan Road joins Highway 3. Turn left onto Highway 3 and ride a short distance into the town of Callahan which has a store, a post office, a lot of history, and little else.

Continue to the east on Highway 3, then 2 miles from Callahan turn left onto Gazelle-Callahan Road and head toward Gazelle. The area between Callahan and Gazelle is half-forested, with some nice vistas. After several miles a climb begins, then a small downhill, and then a climb once again, cresting at Gazelle Mountain Summit (4,921 feet) 15 miles from Callahan. On the other side, an exhilarating serpentine descent lasts for 4 miles (you will be using your brakes). After seven more miles of gentle downslope is the small town of Gazelle with a small store in a gas station. Turn right in Gazelle onto Old 99 Highway.

*Riders using the shortcut route from Siskiyou Pass that began in the previous section join the main route in Gazelle.*

From Gazelle, continue south on Old 99 Highway for 7 miles, cross under Freeway 5, and immediately turn right onto Edgewood Road, which passes over several small hills on its way into Weed. Weed is a nice-sized town to overnight in, with motels and a good selection of restaurants.

## Campgrounds

1. **Bridge Flat Campground.** 17 miles south of Horse Creek on Scott River Road. Has drinking water, swimming. Open 5/1–10/31. Forest Service.

2. **Spring Flat Campground.** 0.5 miles south of campground #1 on Scott River Road. Has drinking water, swimming. Open 5/1–10/31. Forest Service.

3. **Indian Scotty Campground.** 3 miles southeast of campground #1 on Scott River Road. Has drinking water, swimming. Open 5/1–10/31. Forest Service.

4. **Etna Campground.** On Howell Avenue at north end of Etna. Has drinking water, nearby stores. Open 5/1–10/31. Forest Service.

5. **Scott Mountain Campground.** 10 miles southeast of Callahan on Highway 3; a 2,200-foot climb from Callahan. Has drinking water. Open 5/1–10/31. Forest Service.

6. **Tree of Heaven Campground.** On Highway 96, 7 miles west of Freeway 5. Has drinking water. Open all year. Forest Service.

# Weed
# to
# Hat Creek

77 miles • Bicycle With Caution

This area lies between mountain ranges; the Trail has left the Cascade Range and will not officially enter the Sierra Nevada until reaching the Feather River south of Lake Almanor. Snow-covered, 14,162-foot Mt. Shasta dominates the skyline.

Highway 89 is narrow and carries considerable traffic for much of its length to Lake Tahoe, but is included because it is the only logical paved route available. Needless to say, cycling on Highway 89 requires caution, discretion, and the willingness to occasionally ride off on a non-paved shoulder (and possibly stop) should traffic dictate. Logging trucks and large, wide RVs are particular hazards. Try to avoid Highway 89 on weekends and holidays. Perhaps some day the state of California will see fit to add a paved shoulder along this two-lane road.

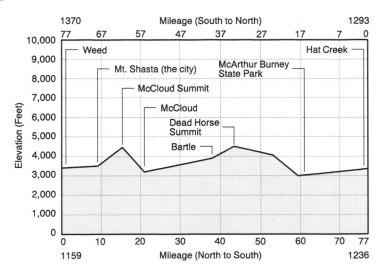

Leave the city of Weed on South Weed Blvd., go under Freeway 5, and continue south as this street becomes a frontage road. Two miles from Weed, enter Freeway 5 and ride on the paved shoulder of the freeway for 2 miles (since a frontage road is not available along this stretch of the freeway). Leave the freeway at the Truck Village exit. Off to the east is Black Butte, a dark, ominous volcanic offshoot of Mt. Shasta.

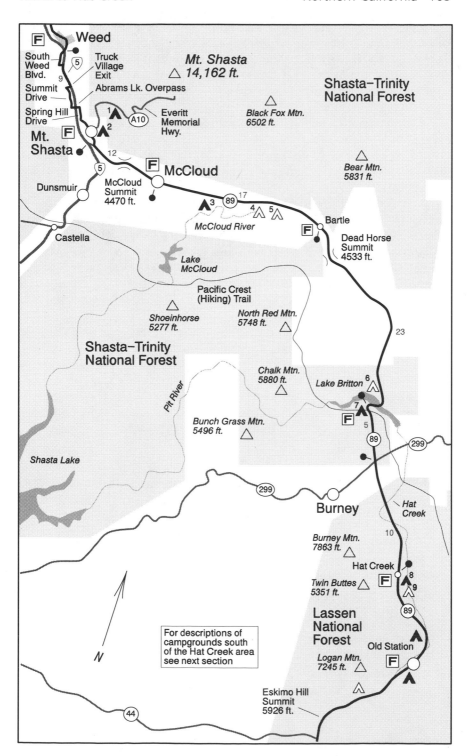

F Weed
South Weed Blvd.
5
Truck Village Exit
9
Summit Drive
Abrams Lk. Overpass
Spring Hill Drive
Mt. Shasta
F
Mt. Shasta △ 14,162 ft.
Black Fox Mtn. 6502 ft.
Shasta–Trinity National Forest

1 ▲
2 ▲
A10
Everitt Memorial Hwy.

12
5
F McCloud
Dunsmuir
McCloud Summit 4470 ft.
89
17
3 ▲
4 ▲ 5 ▲
McCloud River
Bartle
F
Bear Mtn. 5831 ft.

Castella
Lake McCloud
Dead Horse Summit 4533 ft.

Pacific Crest (Hiking) Trail
Shoeinhorse 5277 ft. △
North Red Mtn. 5748 ft. △
23

Shasta–Trinity National Forest
Pit River
Chalk Mtn. 5880 ft. △
Lake Britton
6 ▲
7 ▲
F
5

Bunch Grass Mtn. 5496 ft. △

Shasta Lake
89
299

299
Burney
Hat Creek

Burney Mtn. 7863 ft. △
10

For descriptions of campgrounds south of the Hat Creek area see next section

N

Hat Creek
F
8 ▲
Twin Buttes 5351 ft. △
9 ▲

Lassen National Forest
89
Old Station ▲
Logan Mtn. 7245 ft. △
F
▲

Eskimo Hill Summit 5926 ft.

44

On the west side of Freeway 5, take the Summit Drive frontage road south for 2 miles, then cross over the freeway at the Abrams Lake Overpass. On the east side of the freeway, turn right and take Spring Hill Drive into the city of Mt. Shasta, where Spring Hill Drive becomes North Mt. Shasta Blvd. This town is a pleasant, touristy place at the base of Mt. Shasta, with a bicycle repair shop and many stores.

Continue heading southeast on North Mt. Shasta Blvd. as it becomes Walnut Street. On the south end of town, bear to the left onto South Mt. Shasta Blvd. (if you continue straight, you will cross the freeway again). South Mt. Shasta Blvd. curves to the east and connects with Highway 89. Proceed east on Highway 89.

Five miles from the start of Highway 89, after a 1,000-foot rise, you reach McCloud Summit at an elevation of 4,470 feet. Five miles beyond the summit and downhill is the old lumber company town of McCloud, which is worth a visit. It has a grocery store. Also in this area are splendid views of Mt. Shasta. After McCloud, Highway 89 loses its paved shoulder. Be careful.

Seventeen miles from McCloud (after some up and down stuff) is a gnat's wing of a town called Bartle with a restaurant. Five miles beyond Bartle is Dead Horse Summit at 4,533 feet.

This area is generally well-forested and can be hot. In a flat area 18 miles down from Dead Horse Summit and near Lake Britton is McArthur-Burney Falls State Park (#7), a popular tourist destination with a well-stocked store and fast food joint. The Pacific Crest (Hiking) Trail crosses the highway here.

Continue south on Highway 89 over relatively flat, lightly forested terrain for 16 miles to the town of Hat Creek, which has a store. There are many campgrounds in the vicinity of Hat Creek and Old Station.

## Campgrounds

1. **McBride Springs Campground.** On Everitt Memorial Highway, 4 miles northeast of and 1,500 feet above the city of Mt. Shasta. Has drinking water. Open 5/1–10/31. Forest Service.

2. **Mt. Shasta KOA Kampground.** In the city of Mt. Shasta at 900 North Mt. Shasta Blvd. Has showers, swimming, laundromat, groceries. Open all year. Privately run.

3. **Fowlers Campground.** 6 miles east of McCloud on Highway 89. Has drinking water, swimming. Open 5/1-11/1. Forest Service.

4. **Cattle Camp Campground.** 11 miles east of McCloud on Highway 89. Has no drinking water. Open 5/1–10/31. Forest Service.

5. **Algoma Campground.** 14 miles east of McCloud on Highway 89. Has no drinking water. Open 5/1–10/31. Forest Service.

6. **Dusty Campground.** On north side of Lake Britton on Highway 89. Has swimming; no drinking water. Open 5/1–10/31. Forest Service.

7. **McArthur-Burney Falls State Park.** On south side of Lake Britton on Highway 89. Crowded in peak summer months. The falls are a treat. Has drinking water, swimming, groceries, laundromat. Open all year. State park.

8. **Hat Creek Hereford Campground.** 1 mile off Highway 89 just south of Hat Creek. Has drinking water, showers, primitive swimming in lake. Privately run.

9. **Honn Campground.** On Highway 89, 1 to 2 miles south of Hat Creek. Has no drinking water, but stream water can be purified. Open 4/1–10/31. Forest Service.

Burney Falls at McArthur-Burney Falls State Park.

# Hat Creek
# to
# Lake Almanor

89 miles • Circling a Recently-Active Volcano

This section through Lassen Volcanic National Park goes up and around Lassen Peak, which rises to 10,457 feet. You will reach one of the highest elevations of the Trail, 8,500 feet, on the mountain.

Lassen Peak last erupted in 1914-15, and considerable activity continued until 1921. There are active hot springs and mudpots along the road in the southern part of the park.

The road through the park is closed by snow during the winter months. Occasionally, snow closes the road temporarily as early as September.

After Lassen the Trail dips down to Lake Almanor.

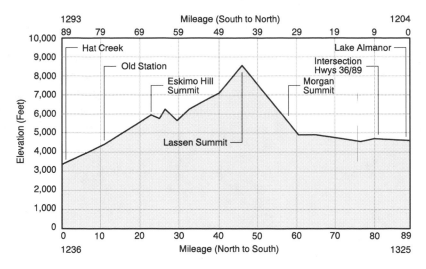

From the town of Hat Creek, gradually climb on Highway 89. There are many logging trucks in this area and no paved shoulder. Be careful. Eleven miles from Hat Creek is Old Station with several food stores.

Now begin climbing in earnest as signs of civilization gradually fall behind. About 12 miles from Old Station you will reach 5,926-foot Eskimo Hill Summit. One mile farther, turn left and follow Highway 89 into Lassen Volcanic National Park.

Manzanita Lake Campground (#6), with a small grocery store, is located 1 mile into the park on the right side of Highway 89. Afterwards, there is a steep 2-mile climb followed by about the same distance downhill. Then there

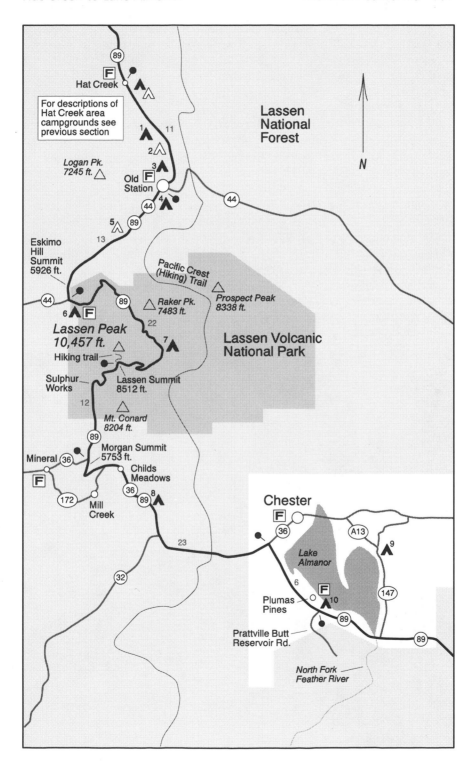

N

**Lassen National Forest**

89

F Hat Creek

For descriptions of Hat Creek area campgrounds see previous section

1 ▲    11
2 △

Logan Pk. 7245 ft. △

3 ▲
Old F
Station

4 ▲

44

89

5 △

13

Eskimo Hill Summit 5926 ft.

Pacific Crest (Hiking) Trail

Prospect Peak 8338 ft. △

44

89    △ Raker Pk. 7483 ft.

6 ▲ F

22

**Lassen Peak 10,457 ft.** △

7 ▲

**Lassen Volcanic National Park**

Hiking trail

Sulphur Works

Lassen Summit 8512 ft.

12    △ Mt. Conard 8204 ft.

89

Morgan Summit 5753 ft.

Mineral 36

F

Childs Meadows

36

172    Mill Creek

89   8 ▲

23

32

**Chester**

F
36

A13

9 ▲

Lake Almanor

147

6

F
Plumas 10 ▲
Pines

89

89

Prattville Butt Reservoir Rd.

North Fork Feather River

are about 17 miles of climbing to Lassen Summit (elevation 8,512 feet). In this section you will pass through a volcanically devastated area where vegetation has just regained a foothold. At Lassen Summit — should you have extra energy to burn — a 2½-mile hiking trail leads to the top of the mountain. Don't be surprised to find snow in shady spots at this elevation well into the summer.

Just past Lassen Summit you will pass a beautiful alpine lake as you begin a long, exhilarating downhill ride through beautiful forests. Seven miles from the summit is the park's south entrance station; five miles beyond that at Morgan Summit is the intersection of Highway 89 and Highway 36. Turn left onto Highway 36/89.

Continue downhill, and as the road levels out 23 miles from Morgan Summit, you arrive at the intersection of Highway 36 and Highway 89 near Lake Almanor, a tourist area. Turn right and continue on Highway 89. (If you wish to visit Chester, the largest city on the lake, continue straight on Highway 36 for 2 miles).

Almanor Campground (#10) is located on Highway 89, 8 miles south of the point where Highway 36 and Highway 89 split, in the vicinity of Plumas Pines and Prattville, and near the intersection of Prattville Butt Reservoir Road and Highway 89. A restaurant and store are nearby.

Mount Lassen as seen from the north.

## Campgrounds

1. **Bridge Campground.** On Highway 89, 6 miles south of Hat Creek. Has drinking water. Open 4/1–10/31. Forest Service.

2. **Rocky Campground.** On Highway 89, 7 miles south of Hat Creek and 3 miles north of Old Station. Has no drinking water. Open 5/15–10/15. Forest Service.

3. **Cave Campground.** On Highway 89, 1 mile north of Old Station. Has flush toilets. Open 4/1–10/31. Forest Service.

4. **Hat Creek Campground.** On Highway 89, 1 mile south of Old Station. Has flush toilets. Open 4/1–10/31. Forest Service.

5. **Big Pine Campground.** On Highway 89, 5 miles south of Old Station. Has no drinking water. Open 5/1–10/31. Forest Service.

6. **Manzanita Lake Campground.** On Highway 89 just inside north entrance of Lassen Volcanic National Park. Has flush toilets, showers, swimming, small grocery store. Open approximately 5/1–9/30. National Park Service.

7. **Summit Lake campgrounds (North and South).** On Highway 89, 13 miles southeast of north entrance to Lassen Volcanic National Park on Highway 89. Has flush toilets, swimming. Open approximately 6/1–9/30. National Park Service.

8. **Gurnsey Creek Campground.** On Highway 36/89, 5 miles southeast of Childs Meadows. Has drinking water. Open 5/1–9/30. Forest Service.

9. **Big Cove Resort.** 9 miles southeast of Chester on east side of Lake Almanor at 442 Peninsula Drive. Has showers, swimming. Open 5/1–10/31. Privately run.

10. **Almanor Campground.** On Highway 89, 8 miles south of the intersection of Highway 36 and Highway 89, and near the towns of Plumas Pines, Prattville, and Lake Almanor. Also near intersection of Highway 89 and Prattville Butt Reservoir Road. Has drinking water, swimming. Open 6/1–10/31. Forest Service.

# Lake Almanor
# to
# Cottonwood Campground

<u>88 miles</u>  •  <u>Entering the Sierra Nevada</u>

The first 25 of these 87 miles is downhill; most of the remainder is gently uphill. Early on, the Trail passes through picturesque canyons on its way to Quincy; later, the Middle Fork of the Feather River and the Union Pacific Railroad run alongside the route near Graeagle. At the end of this section, Lake Tahoe is tantalizingly close.

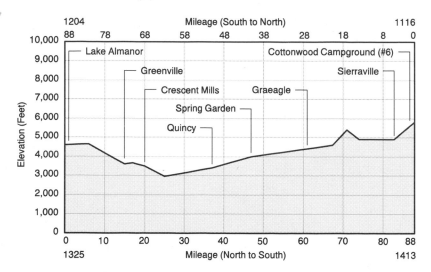

From Almanor Campground, it is 6 miles south on Highway 89 to the intersection of Highway 89 and Highway 147. From there it is 9 miles south and downhill on Highway 89 to Greenville. Greenville, the largest town between Lake Almanor and Quincy, has a number of stores and a restaurant.

About 5 miles past Greenville is Crescent Mills with a store and restaurant. Past Crescent Mills, follow Highway 89 seven miles down a beautiful river canyon to the intersection of Highway 89 and Highway 70. Turn left, remaining on Highway 89, and proceed uphill past a spring. Eleven miles beyond the intersection of the highways is the prosperous city of Quincy, a city of 5,000 nestled in a mountain valley.

From Quincy, continue climbing gently southeast on Highway 89 for 10 miles to the tiny town of Spring Garden, which has a country store. In this area Highway 89 slowly rises as it begins to follow the Middle Fork of the Feather River. Continue to watch for speeding logging trucks.

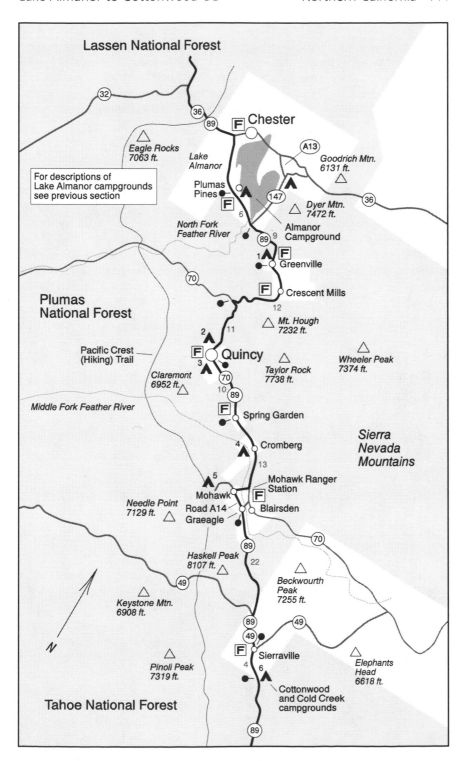

Lassen National Forest

32

36
89   F Chester

Eagle Rocks
7063 ft.        Lake
Almanor                              A13

Goodrich Mtn.
6131 ft.

For descriptions of
Lake Almanor campgrounds
see previous section

Plumas
Pines          F          147          36

6                                      Dyer Mtn.
7472 ft.

North Fork
Feather River                Almanor
Campground

89  9

1      F

70                              Greenville

F      Crescent Mills

12

Plumas                                  Mt. Hough
National Forest                          7232 ft.

2      11                              Wheeler Peak
7374 ft.

Pacific Crest        F
(Hiking) Trail      3      Quincy

Claremont                             Taylor Rock
6952 ft.         70                    7738 ft.
10
89

Middle Fork Feather River

F      Spring Garden

Sierra
Nevada
Mountains

4      Cromberg

13

5                   Mohawk Ranger
Station
Mohawk          F
Needle Point
7129 ft.        Road A14          Blairsden
Graeagle

89                    70

Haskell Peak
8107 ft.                  22

49                              Beckwourth
Peak
7255 ft.

Keystone Mtn.
6908 ft.

N

89

49

49

Pinoli Peak                   F      Sierraville
7319 ft.                 4      6           Elephants
Head
6618 ft.

Cottonwood
and Cold Creek
campgrounds
Tahoe National Forest

89

About 12 miles from Spring Garden, before reaching Blairsden, turn right at the Mohawk Ranger Station onto Little Bear Road and ride across the new bridge to the first intersection. To go to Plumas Eureka State Park (#5) turn right on Road A14; otherwise, turn left onto Road A14 and proceed into Mohawk, which has a store, restaurant, and motel. Continue on this road to Graeagle, a recreation locale with a golf course and a lot of old folks. This is a good place for a mid-day lunch stop.

After Graeagle, connect with Highway 89 again and head south as the highway meanders gently upward for 7 miles with close-in trees and shade before beginning a 4-mile climb to a 5,441-foot summit. After coasting 3 miles down, you will have 8 more miles to Sierraville across a broad, flat valley. This small town has a store, a restaurant and lots of traffic because Highway 49 passes through.

It is another uphill pull after Sierraville on Highway 89 into Tahoe National Forest. Cold Creek and Cottonwood campgrounds (#6) are about 4 miles south of and close to 1,000 feet above Sierraville. Many other campgrounds lie between Sierraville and Lake Tahoe if you are willing to push further.

### Campgrounds

1. **Greenville Campground.** On Highway 89, 0.5 mile north of Greenville. Has drinking water, swimming. Open 5/1–10/31. County park.

2. **Rockwell Park Campground.** On Highway 89, 2 miles northeast of Quincy. Has flush toilets, swimming. Open 5/1–10/31. County park.

3. **Plumas County Campground.** On Highway 89, at east end of Quincy. Next to fairgrounds; near stores, restaurants. Has flush toilets. County park.

4. **Jackson Creek Campground.** On Highway 89 near Cromberg. Has flush toilets. Open 5/1–10/31. Forest Service.

5. **Plumas Eureka State Park.** On County Road A14, 4 miles southwest of Mohawk. Open 6/11–9/6. State park.

6. **Cold Creek and Cottonwood campgrounds.** On Highway 89 about 4 miles southeast of Sierraville. Together they offer a lot of tent-RV spaces. Both have drinking water. Open 5/1–10/31. Forest Service.

Logging trucks are frequently encountered along the Trail. Carrying 30 to 35 tons of logs, they are difficult to stop quickly. Give them your full respect.

# Cottonwood Campground
# to
# South Lake Tahoe

63 miles • The Jewel of the Sierra Nevada

From Cottonwood Campground near Sierraville it is 20 miles to Truckee and 35 miles to Lake Tahoe. Once you reach Lake Tahoe, beautifully ringed with high mountains, you will know you are in the Sierra Nevada.

Lake Tahoe is 22 miles long and 10 miles wide at its widest point. A ride around the lake is a good day's jaunt of 74 miles.

Campgrounds near or on Lake Tahoe are usually full during the summer months. Consider using Kaspian Campground (#9) or a motel in South Lake Tahoe.

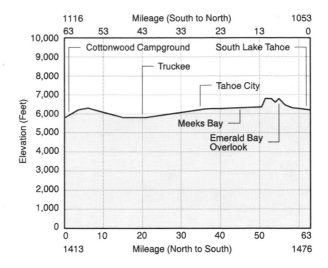

Bicycle south on Highway 89 from Cottonwood Campground. Fifteen miles from the campground is the turnoff for the Prosser Lake campgrounds (#4). One mile beyond is the site where many lives were lost when the Donner wagon train was stranded in the snows of 1846. A few years later in 1849, some 40,000 "49ers" used Donner Pass on their way to California gold fields.

Two miles after the Donner site, cross over Freeway 80; a sign will say you are now on Highway 267. Follow the road a short distance to the first stop sign in Truckee. Do not turn left to follow Highway 267; it is much easier to reach Lake Tahoe via Highway 89. Instead, turn right onto Bridge Street and bike about one block to a left turn onto Jibboom Street. After about two blocks, turn left onto Spring Street, bike one block, then turn right onto Donner Pass Road.

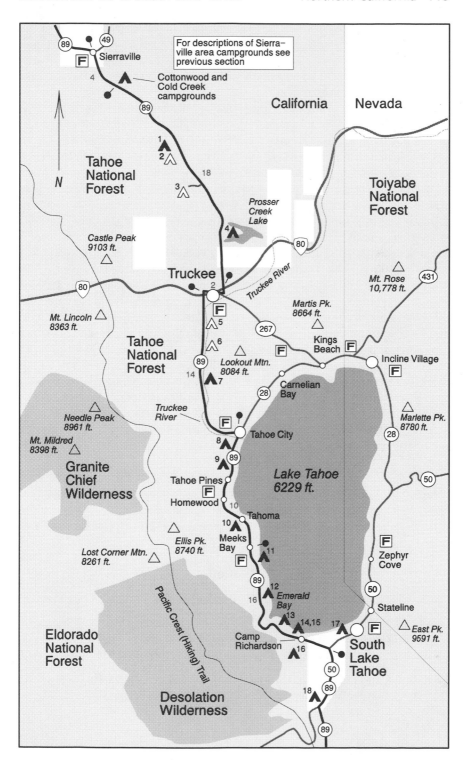

Truckee is an active little town with considerable tourist trade and plenty of stores and restaurants. Ride on Donner Pass Road through the Truckee business strip, pass under Freeway 80, and finally turn left onto Highway 89 near a Safeway store. Just ahead you pass under Freeway 80 again and Lake Tahoe is 14 miles ahead.

The portion of the highway from Truckee to the Squaw Valley turnoff is wide, with a bike lane and gradual upward gradient that makes biking a real pleasure. There are many campgrounds along this stretch of highway.

Nine miles from Truckee, Highway 89 narrows but fortunately a short distance later a well-kept, paved bike path begins and continues into Tahoe City. You will probably see people merrily rafting down the Truckee River, which runs alongside the path. In Tahoe City, where you will get your first glimpse of Lake Tahoe, turn right onto West Lake Blvd. (Highway 89) and head south on the bike path. Watch out for novice cyclists along this stretch of homes, restaurants, and stores which lasts until D.L. Bliss State Park.

During the summer months the west shore of Lake Tahoe is busy and after biking through country areas, bumper-to-bumper traffic can seem strange. Kaspian Campground (#9) on this stretch is specifically designated for bicyclists and hikers; other campgrounds on the lake are often full during the summer months and officials frown on sleeping on the beaches.

The Trail is relatively level until you reach D.L. Bliss State Park about 15 miles south of Tahoe City on Highway 89. Here, a steep 2-mile pull begins that takes you up to a stunning view of Emerald Bay. Along the way, watch out for rubbernecking auto drivers. The 2-mile downhill with switchbacks on the other side is steep at first. Check your brakes before descending. After reaching flat terrain, a 4-mile bicycle trail paralleling Highway 89 lasts until the intersection of Highway 50 and Highway 89. To go into the city of South Lake Tahoe follow Highway 50 to the left.

Seriously consider staying in a motel in South Lake Tahoe if you want to sample the gambling and entertainment just over the border in Nevada, or just want to rest up a bit. To draw free-spending customers, the major casinos offer inexpensive and expansive all-you-can-eat buffets along with free transportation from most South Lake Tahoe motels.

### Campgrounds

*The closer a campground is to Lake Tahoe, the greater the chance that it will be full during the summer months.*

1. **Lower Little Truckee Campground.** On Highway 89, 8 miles southeast of Sierraville. Has drinking water. Open 5/1–11/30. Forest Service.

2. **Upper Little Truckee Campground.** On Highway 89, 10 miles southeast of Sierraville. Has drinking water. Open 5/1–11/30. Forest Service.

3. **Sagehen Creek Campground.** 9 miles northwest of Truckee on Highway 89, then 2 miles west on Forest Road 18N11 (Sagehen Road). Has no drinking water. Open 5/1–10/31. Forest Service.

4. **Prosser, Annie McCloud, and Lakeside campgrounds.** All are approximately 5 miles north of Truckee off Highway 89 at Prosser Lake. Only Prosser Campground has drinking water. Swimming available at the lake. Open 5/1–10/31. Forest Service.

5. **Granite Flat Campground.** On Highway 89, 3 miles south of Truckee. Has no drinking water, but water from the Truckee River can be purified. Open 4/1–10/31. Forest Service.

6. **Goose Meadow Campground.** On Highway 89, 6 miles south of Truckee. Has no drinking water, but water from the Truckee River can be purified. Open 5/1–10/31. Forest Service.

7. **Silver Creek Campground.** On Highway 89, 9 miles south of Truckee. Has drinking water. Open 5/1–10/31. Forest Service.

8. **William Kent Campground.** On Highway 89, 2 miles south of Tahoe City. Has flush toilets. Open 6/1–9/30. Forest Service.

9. **Kaspian Campground.** On Highway 89, 4 miles south of Tahoe City. Reserved for cyclists and hikers. Has flush toilets. Open 5/1–9/30. Forest Service.

10. **General Creek Campground.** In Sugar Pine Point State Park on Highway 89, 1 mile south of Tahoma. Has flush toilets. Open all year. State park.

11. **Meeks Bay Campground.** On Highway 89 in the town of Meeks Bay. Has flush toilets. Open 6/1–9/30. Forest Service.

12. **D.L. Bliss State Park Campground.** On Highway 89, 6 miles south of Meeks Bay. Has flush toilets. Open 5/1–9/30. State park.

13. **Emerald Bay State Park, Eagle Point Campground.** On Highway 89, 8 miles north of South Lake Tahoe. Has flush toilets. Open 6/1–8/31. State park.

14. **Camp Shelly Campground.** Off Highway 89, 2 miles west of the town of Camp Richardson. Has flush toilets, showers. Open 6/1–9/30. Municipal park.

15. **Camp Richardson Resort.** Off Highway 89, 0.5 mile north of the town of Camp Richardson. Has flush toilets, showers. Open 6/1–10/31. Forest Service.

16. **Fallen Leaf Campground.** Off Highway 89, 2 miles southwest of the town of Camp Richardson. Has flush toilets. Open 5/1–10/31. Forest Service.

17. **South Lake Tahoe El Dorado Campground.** In downtown South Lake Tahoe at the intersection of Highway 50 and Rufus Allen Blvd. Reservations are recommended. Has flush toilets, showers. Open 4/1–10/31. Municipal park.

18. **KOA Kampground of South Lake Tahoe.** Near intersection of Highway 50 and Highway 89 in Myers. Has flush toilets, showers, store. Open 6/1–9/31. Privately run.

# Region 4
# Central California

Yosemite Valley and Bridalveil Falls in the winter.

# South Lake Tahoe
# to
# Chris Flat Campground

## 72 miles • Conquering Monitor Pass

After the relatively easy riding between Lake Almanor and Lake Tahoe, you begin serious climbing with Monitor Pass. The Trail now switches to the east side of the Sierra Nevada, which has an entirely different look.

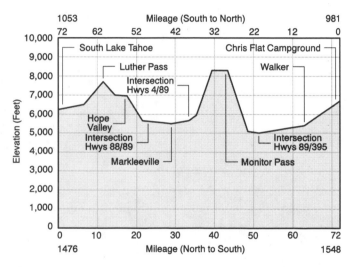

Leave South Lake Tahoe via Highway 50/89 and head south past the Tahoe airport. After 5 miles leave Highway 50 and turn left onto Highway 89. About 7 miles beyond, and 1,300 feet higher, is the top of Luther Pass. By the time your reach the meadows of Hope Valley on the other side, all the glitz of Tahoe has evaporated. The valley is unspoiled, unpopulated, and beautiful. At the intersection with Highway 88, turn left onto Highway 88/89, and after about 1 mile there is a restaurant and lodging.

Staying on Highway 88/89, cross a bridge and begin a long downhill through a strikingly beautiful canyon with a number of campgrounds (#1), some near a sparkling mountain stream. Down and out of the canyon, turn right to stay on Highway 89 as Highway 88 departs to thread its way into Nevada. A store and restaurant are available 0.5 mile east on Highway 88 at the town of Woodfords.

On Highway 89, 7 miles from the intersection of Highway 88 and Highway 89, is the friendly little town of Markleeville with a store or two. Markleeville is the county seat of Alpine County, the least populated of

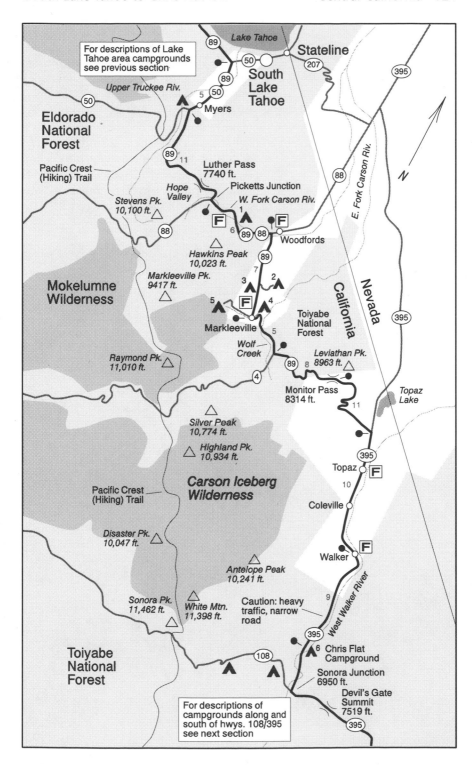

For descriptions of Lake Tahoe area campgrounds see previous section

Lake Tahoe

Stateline

South Lake Tahoe

Upper Truckee Riv.

Myers

Eldorado National Forest

Pacific Crest (Hiking) Trail

Luther Pass 7740 ft.

Hope Valley

Picketts Junction

W. Fork Carson Riv.

Stevens Pk. 10,100 ft.

Woodfords

E. Fork Carson Riv.

Nevada

California

Mokelumne Wilderness

Hawkins Peak 10,023 ft.

Markleeville Pk. 9417 ft.

Markleeville

Toiyabe National Forest

Wolf Creek

Leviathan Pk. 8963 ft.

Raymond Pk. 11,010 ft.

Monitor Pass 8314 ft.

Topaz Lake

Silver Peak 10,774 ft.

Highland Pk. 10,934 ft.

Carson Iceberg Wilderness

Pacific Crest (Hiking) Trail

Topaz

Coleville

Disaster Pk. 10,047 ft.

Walker

Antelope Peak 10,241 ft.

West Walker River

Sonora Pk. 11,462 ft.

White Mtn. 11,398 ft.

Caution: heavy traffic, narrow road

Toiyabe National Forest

Chris Flat Campground

Sonora Junction 6950 ft.

Devil's Gate Summit 7519 ft.

For descriptions of campgrounds along and south of hwys. 108/395 see next section

California's counties with only 1,200 people. It is also the beginning for the annual Markleeville Death Ride (for cyclists).

Four miles off on a side road from Markleeville is Grover Hot Springs State Park (#5), a popular place for its hot spring-fed pool which does wonders for sore muscles. Realize though, that you may want to stay for days! Bicyclists are assigned to camp in a day-use area and do not need reservations.

From Markleeville to the intersection of Highway 89 and Highway 4 the road climbs gently uphill for 5 miles, but things change dramatically when you turn left to stay on Highway 89. Here begins the 6-mile, 2,500-foot climb through canyons to the 4-mile-long, breezy, and lonely plateau that leads to Monitor Pass. This is one of the tougher climbs on the Pacific Crest Bicycle Trail.

View across the windy plateau near Monitor Pass.

Here, the east side of the Sierra Nevada is dry, with sparse vegetation — most of the rain and snow is captured by the western slopes. The 8-mile, 8-percent downhill after Monitor Pass is long and serpentine with great views into the flats and nearby mountains of Nevada and California. You will pass down a narrow and quite beautiful canyon just before connecting with Highway 395. At this point we bid a sad farewell to good (or bad) old Highway 89, which carried us all the way from Mt. Shasta.

Turn right onto Highway 395 and ride the 10 level miles through Topaz (has a store) and Coleville to the town of Walker, which is located on the West Walker River. Walker, which lies at the end of Antelope Valley, has at least one store and several restaurants. Be careful: portions of Highway 395 between Coleville and Bootleg Campground (#6) are dangerous due to the narrow road and speeding traffic. Be extremely wary of wide trucks and RVs — do not tempt fate. Stay as far right as possible, do not ride in poor light, and leave the road if necessary.

Bootleg Campground, on the West Walker River, is about 8 miles south of Walker, and Chris Flat Campground (#6) is 1 mile beyond.

## Campgrounds

1. **Kit Carson, Snowshoe Springs, and Crystal Springs campgrounds.** On Highway 89 and the Carson River, in the canyon between the edge of Hope Valley and the intersection of Highway 88 and Highway 89. All have drinking water. Open 6/1–10/31. Forest Service.

2. **Indian Creek Reservoir Campground.** 3 miles north of Markleeville on Highway 89, then 4 miles on Airport Road. Has flush toilets and showers. Open 5/1–9/30. Bureau of Land Management.

3. **Turtle Rock Park Campground.** On Highway 89, 3 miles north of Markleeville. Has flush toilets. Open 5/1–9/30. County park.

4. **Markleeville Campground.** On Highway 89, 1 mile north of Markleeville. Has drinking water. Open 5/1–10/31. Forest Service.

5. **Grover Hot Springs State Park.** On County Road E1, 4 miles west of Markleeville. Has an area reserved for bicyclists, and has showers, swimming, hot spring. Food is available in Markleeville. Open all year. State park.

6. **Bootleg and Chris Flat campgrounds.** On Highway 395 and West Walker River about 8 and 9 miles, respectively, south of Walker. Both have drinking water; only Bootleg has flush toilets. Open 5/1–10/31. Forest Service.

# Chris Flat Campground
# to
# Tuolumne Meadows

68 miles • Over Tioga Pass Into Yosemite's High Country

After two small summits and a 3,000-foot climb, the Trail hits the highest point of its 2,500-mile length at Tioga Pass, the entrance to Yosemite National Park. The high Sierra country beyond the pass has a flavor all its own. Be prepared for cold weather at this elevation.

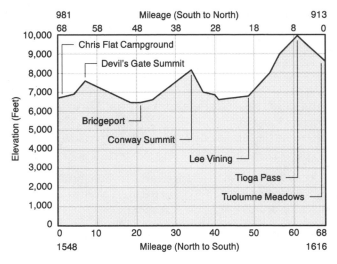

From Chris Flat Campground, bike 4 miles south to Sonora Junction (the intersection of Highway 395 and Highway 108). The landscape again is treeless, with rolling hills and grazing sheep. Three miles beyond Sonora Junction on Highway 395 you reach 7,519-foot Devils Gate Summit. Afterwards, enjoy an 11-mile downhill, then ride 3 miles across grassy Bridgeport Valley to the prosperous town of Bridgeport. Two campgrounds are located on the nearby lake.

From Bridgeport it is approximately 13 miles up wide Highway 395 to 8,138-foot Conway Summit. Then it is down a 4-lane, 6-percent grade for 3 miles. Fourteen miles from Conway Summit is the town of Lee Vining with several stores and a large restaurant. Do not overeat and overdrink if you intend to climb Tioga Pass the same day.

You have passed Mono Lake which lies to the east of Highway 395. There is an information center in Lee Vining where you can learn about the city of

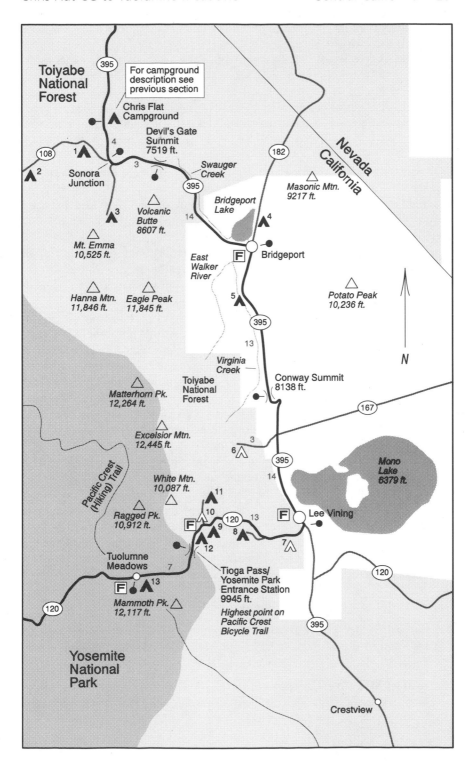

Toiyabe National Forest

For campground description see previous section

Chris Flat Campground

Devil's Gate Summit 7519 ft.

Swauger Creek

Masonic Mtn. 9217 ft.

Sonora Junction

Bridgeport Lake

Bridgeport

Volcanic Butte 8607 ft.

East Walker River

Mt. Emma 10,525 ft.

Potato Peak 10,236 ft.

Hanna Mtn. 11,846 ft.

Eagle Peak 11,845 ft.

Virginia Creek

Conway Summit 8138 ft.

Matterhorn Pk. 12,264 ft.

Toiyabe National Forest

Excelsior Mtn. 12,445 ft.

Mono Lake 6379 ft.

Pacific Crest (Hiking) Trail

White Mtn. 10,087 ft.

Ragged Pk. 10,912 ft.

Lee Vining

Tuolumne Meadows

Tioga Pass/ Yosemite Park Entrance Station 9945 ft.

Mammoth Pk. 12,117 ft.

Highest point on Pacific Crest Bicycle Trail

Yosemite National Park

Crestview

Nevada
California

N

Los Angeles causing the lake to shrink by diverting for its own use a large amount of the lake's tributary waters.

Mono Lake is highly alkaline and gets more so as its water evaporates. The odd "tufa" formations along the shore are mineral deposits that have been exposed by the lowering of the water level. When the lake gets too low, the gulls that raise young on protected islands in the lake are exposed to predators. The dark island in the center of the lake is a volcanic cone. This area of California, especially to the south in the area of Bishop, is seismically active.

But we will not take Highway 395 to Bishop. Instead, on Highway 395 just south of Lee Vining, turn your trusty handlebars west. Do not take the first right turn — it's too steep — instead, take the second right turn and head toward Tioga Pass on Highway 120. You are facing a climb of about 3,000 feet.

Head up a valley which has several campgrounds. High mountains, often capped with snow, loom ahead, and you will breathe deeply in thinning air as you climb. Stops to absorb the scenery and take in some liquid refreshment will give you new bursts of energy along the way.

Nine miles from Lee Vining is the 9,000-foot level. Two miles later you will have finished the toughest part of the climb. At this point there is a store and lodging. If you are travelling early or late in the year, this will be the last place to buy food until you reach Yosemite Valley because the Tuolumne Meadows store and restaurant will be closed. Two miles beyond the store and somewhat uphill is 9,945-foot Tioga Pass and the entrance to Yosemite National Park pictured on the cover of this book. Get in line with the cars. You will be provided with all kinds of printed information and you will pay a small fee compared to what motorists must pay.

Here you truly have the feeling that you are high up — often there will be snow remaining at this elevation into the summer.

After the entrance station, the route drops 900 feet over 7 miles on Highway 120 (Tioga Pass Road) to Tuolumne (Too-AH-lum-ee) Meadows, the largest meadow in the Sierra Nevada. The Pacific Crest (Hiking) Trail crosses here, and the store and restaurant are great gathering points for the young crowd. You will see rock-climbing enthusiasts, backpackers, day-trip cyclists, and various wild and woolly types.

## Campgrounds

1. **Sonora Bridge Campground.** On Highway 108, 2 miles northwest of the intersection of Highway 395 and Highway 108. Has drinking water. Open 5/1–10/31. Forest Service.

2. **Leavitt Meadows Campground.** On Highway 108, 6 miles west of the intersection of Highway 395 and Highway 108. Has drinking water. Open 5/1–10/31. Forest Service.

3. **Obsidian Campground.** About 1 mile southeast of Sonora Junction on Highway 395, then 4 miles south on Forest Road 10066. May be a tough ride for non-mountain-type bikes. Has drinking water. Open 5/1–10/31. Forest Service.

4. **Paradise Shores Trailer Park and Falling Rock Marina RV Park.** Both are 2 miles north of Bridgeport on Highway 182 at Bridgeport Lake. Both have drinking water, laundromats. Paradise Shores has showers. Both open 4/25–10/31. Privately run.

5. **Willow Springs Trailer Park.** On Highway 395, 5 miles south of Bridgeport. Has drinking water, laundromat. Open 4/25–10/21. Privately run.

6. **Mill Creek County Park.** 8 miles north of Lee Vining, then 3 miles west on Lundy Lake Road. Has no drinking water. Open 5/1–10/31. County park.

7. **Lee Vining Creek County Park.** On Highway 120, 1 mile south of Lee Vining. Has no drinking water. Open 5/1–10/31. County park.

8. **Big Bend Campground.** 3 miles west of Lee Vining on Highway 120, then 3 miles west on Road 1N21. Has drinking water. Open 4/25–11/1. Forest Service.

*The opening dates for the following campgrounds vary from year to year depending on snow conditions.*

9. **Ellery Lake Campground.** On Highway 120, 9 miles west of Lee Vining. Has drinking water. Open 6/1–10/15. Forest Service.

10. **Junction Campground.** 10 miles west of Lee Vining off Highway 120 on Road 1N04. Has no drinking water. Open 6/1–10/15. Forest Service.

11. **Saddlebag Lake Campground.** 10 miles west of Lee Vining on Highway 120, then 2 miles northwest on Road 1N04. Has flush toilets. Open 6/1–10/15. Forest Service.

12. **Tioga Lake Campground.** On Highway 120, 11 miles west of Lee Vining. Has drinking water. Open 6/1–10/15. Forest Service.

13. **Tuolumne Meadows Campground.** 8 miles west of Yosemite National Park's Tioga Pass Entrance Station. Has drinking water, restaurant, store, post office. Open 6/10–10/15. National Park Service.

# Tuolumne Meadows
# to
# Yosemite Valley

53 miles • Grandeur in an Overpopulated Valley

This section is short and easy with lots of coasting, allowing you time to make camp in Yosemite Valley and enjoy the sights and facilities there.

Glacially-formed Yosemite Valley with its spectacular waterfalls and magnificent canyon walls is one of the wonders of the world; the drawback is the overabundance of tourists, cars, and even smog. The information you received at the park entrance will tell you more about the natural history of the park and what there is to see and do. One campground in Yosemite Valley is reserved for visitors (backpackers and cyclists) who arrive under their own power.

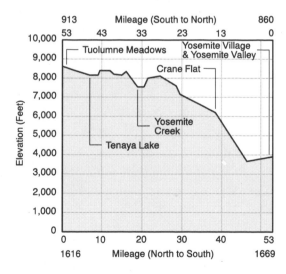

At the higher elevations in the park it usually gets cold, often dipping to freezing at night. You will likely need to wear gloves if you are riding from Tuolumne Meadows early in the morning. Remember that Highway 120 (Tioga Pass Road) is closed each winter due to snow. Also the thinner air at this altitude will cause you to breathe heavier.

Highway 120 is on the narrow side — fortunately no heavy trucks are allowed. It is 7 miles generally downhill from Tuolumne Meadows to Tenaya Lake. After the lake there is a small climb, then after some up-and-down work and shortly after the turnoff to Porcupine Flat Campground (#2) is a 3-mile

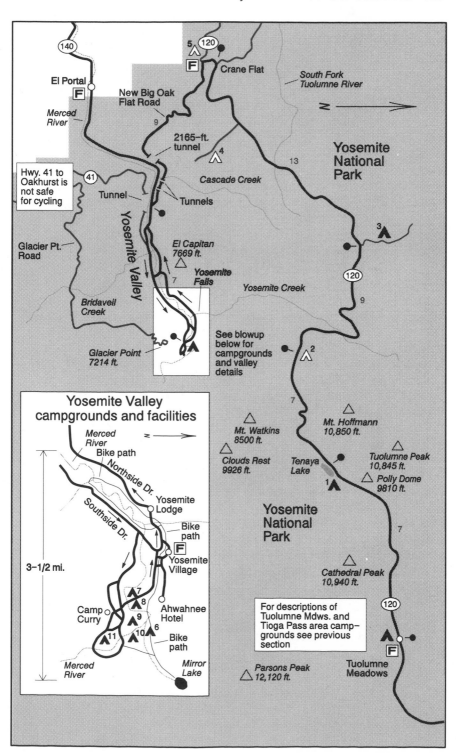

140

5
120
F
Crane Flat

El Portal
F

New Big Oak
Flat Road

Merced
River

9

2165–ft.
tunnel

4

South Fork
Tuolumne River

Yosemite
National
Park

13

Hwy. 41 to
Oakhurst is
not safe
for cycling

41

Tunnel

Tunnels

Cascade Creek

Glacier Pt.
Road

Yosemite Valley

El Capitan
7669 ft.

Yosemite
Falls

3

120

Yosemite Creek

9

Bridaveil
Creek

7

Glacier Point
7214 ft.

See blowup
below for
campgrounds
and valley
details

2

7

Yosemite Valley
campgrounds and facilities

Merced
River

Bike path

Northside Dr.

Mt. Watkins
8500 ft.

Mt. Hoffmann
10,850 ft.

Clouds Rest
9926 ft.

Tuolumne Peak
10,845 ft.

Southside Dr.

Yosemite
Lodge

Bike
path

F

Yosemite
Village

Tenaya
Lake

1

Polly Dome
9810 ft.

Yosemite
National
Park

3-1/2 mi.

7

Camp
Curry

8

9

Ahwahnee
Hotel

6

10

Bike
path

11

Cathedral Peak
10,940 ft.

120

For descriptions of
Tuolumne Mdws. and
Tioga Pass area camp-
grounds see previous
section

F

Merced
River

Mirror
Lake

Parsons Peak
12,120 ft.

Tuolumne
Meadows

downhill to Yosemite Creek, the stream that eventually cascades into Yosemite Valley as Yosemite Falls. Next is a 4-mile climb on Highway 120 ending at the turnoff to White Wolf Campground (#3).

Now the fun begins. For the next 13 miles to Crane Flat Junction (where there is a store and restrooms), you will whiz through beautiful woods as you descend 2,000 feet. At Crane Flat Junction turn left onto New Big Oak Flat Road and descend another 2,500 feet over 9 miles. You will have your first spectacular views of the valley on the way down.

You will want to keep a close eye on traffic and brake judiciously to avoid getting down to the valley the fast way — over the edge of the roadway, which is cut into the steep walls of the valley. There are parking spots and scenic outlooks on the way down. You will also pass through three tunnels — the first is a half-mile long and the other two are short. If you have lights on the rear of your bike turn them on at least during the long tunnel. Be careful!

At the end of the downhill you will intersect Highway 140. To reach the heart of Yosemite Valley, turn left onto Highway 140, ride 1 mile on Northside Drive, then turn right and cross over the Merced River. (Signs explain where to go.) At the next intersection turn left onto Southside Drive and ride 4 miles to the center of the tourist facilities. On your way there you may wish to stop to see Bridalveil Falls, a short distance off Southside Drive.

Be aware that many of the roads in the valley are one-way in order to cope with heavy summer traffic. There has been talk about limiting the number of cars in the valley.

There are three major visitor areas at the east end of Yosemite Valley: Yosemite Village, Curry Village, and the Yosemite Lodge area. Yosemite Village has the general store and post office.

As mentioned previously, if you are bicycle touring, you can automatically use the Backpacker's Campground (#6). Make reservations in advance if you intend to use other park accommodations — everything from the upscale Ahwahnee Hotel to tents on wooden platforms are available.

Things to do in Yosemite Valley include a visit to the base of Yosemite Falls (the flow diminishes as the year progresses), a hike to Vernal Falls, and a bicycle ride to Mirror Lake on a bike trail. If you have the energy, hike to the top of Yosemite Falls (if the trail is open) or Half Dome. There are many possibilities for backpacking trips out of Yosemite Valley if you can find a place to keep your bike.

The last time I visited Yosemite, there were daily bus trips between Merced, California and Yosemite Lodge. This may be useful if you are beginning or ending your trip in Yosemite.

### Campgrounds

1. **Tenaya Lake Campground.** On Highway 120, 7 miles west of Tuolumne Meadows. Open approximately 6/10–10/30. Has drinking water, no showers. National Park Service.

2. **Porcupine Flat Campground** On Highway 120, 15 miles west of Tuolumne Meadows. Open approximately 6/10–10/15. Has no drinking water. National Park Service.

3. **White Wolf Campground.** 24 miles west of Tuolumne Meadows on Highway 120, then 1 mile north of highway. Open approximately 6/10–10/15. Has drinking water; a grocery store and restaurant are open during peak tourist months. National Park Service.

4. **Tamarack Flat Campground.** 5 miles southwest of White Wolf Campground on Highway 120, then 4 miles off highway. Open approximately 6/10–10/15. Has no drinking water. National Park Service.

5. **Crane Flat Campground.** Near intersection of Highway 120 and New Big Oak Flat Road. Open approximately 5/26–10/1. Has drinking water. National Park Service.

*The following campgrounds are located in the same general area of Yosemite Valley. All have drinking water; a store and a restaurant are located in Yosemite Village. At least one camp in the area is open year around. Refer to the valley map for exact locations. All are managed by the National Park Service.*

6. **Backpacker's Campground.** Reserved for backpackers and touring bicyclists.

7. **Lower River Campground.**

8. **Upper River Campground.**

9. **Lower Pines Campground.**

10. **North Pines Campground.**

11. **Upper Pines Campground.**

# Yosemite Valley
# to
# Bass Lake

83 miles • Moving Into the Southern Sierra Nevada

Now that you are on the western slopes of the Sierra Nevada you will see more forests. Unfortunately, in some areas the lack of high-elevation roads forces the Trail into foothills which can be hot during the daytime. From here on, get started as early as possible during the summer months.

Do not use Highway 41 from Yosemite Valley south toward Bass Lake — it is very narrow in spots and is heavily used by RVs from the Los Angeles area. Instead follow the Merced River Canyon and Highway 140 to Briceburg, where you begin crossing a series of low-elevation ridges and branches of the Chowchilla River between the towns of Mariposa and Ahwahnee.

Beyond Oakhurst, the Trail climbs to Bass Lake with its many campgrounds.

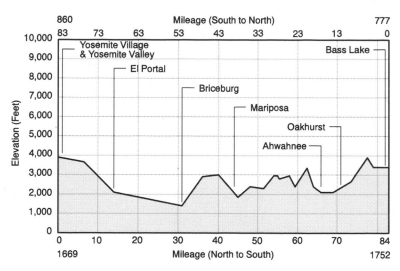

Bicycle out of Yosemite Valley and west on Highway 140. It is 12 miles from Yosemite Village to the west entrance of Yosemite National Park. About 3 miles beyond the entrance and just outside the park boundary is the town of El Portal with stores and motels. From El Portal follow Highway 140 seventeen miles down the geologically interesting Merced River Canyon to the micro-town of Briceburg, which has a small food store.

Beyond Briceburg, continue on Highway 140 as it leaves the Merced River and begin the first work of the day, climbing for 9 miles to Midpines Summit.

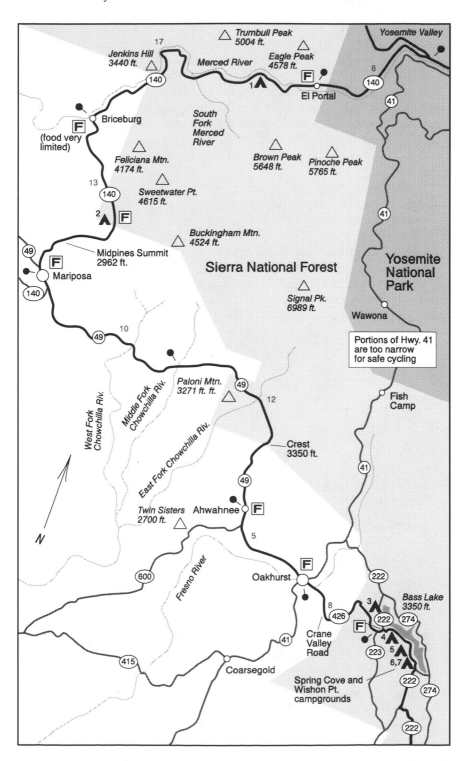

From the summit it is a 4-mile coast into Mariposa, a prosperous, historical city reminiscent of Truckee, except smaller, with stores, motels, and restaurants. Down at this elevation (1,950 feet) the days really heat up during the summer — up into the 90s.

In Mariposa connect with Highway 49 (named after the gold-seeking 49ers) and head southeast. You will encounter a series of hills or ridges in semi-arid countryside. A net 1,000-foot gain in elevation leads to a 500-foot drop to a bridge over the East Fork of the Chowchilla River, then a 900-foot climb to the top of a ridge which marks the Madera County line, 18 miles from Mariposa.

At the county line the extra-wide road narrows, followed by a downhill ride through Ahwahnee, which has a grocery store. Five miles past Ahwahnee is prosperous Oakhurst, with stores, motels, and a small, shady park next to the town library.

In Oakhurst, turn left onto Highway 41 (the city's main street), then after a short distance turn right onto Road 426 at a stop sign and ride past the post office.

From Oakhurst there is a substantial 6-mile climb past residences on Road 426 to the top of a ridge overlooking Bass Lake. The first time I rode this route, I figured that the ride from Oakhurst to Bass Lake had to be downhill. Wrong. Bass Lake is a man-made reservoir in the hills. From the top of the ridge, ride downhill a mile or so on the somewhat steep Road 426 to the lake. There is a food store (Forks Resort) at the intersection of Road 426 and Road 222. Finally, turn right and ride 4 miles on Highway 222 to Wishon Point Campground (#7) on the southern end of the lake.

All of the public campgrounds at Bass Lake are on the west side. The attractive lake is popular, so reservations during the summer are advised.

## Campgrounds

1. **Indian Flat Campground.** On Highway 140, 4 miles west of El Portal. Has drinking water. Open 7/15–9/15. Forest Service.

2. **Yosemite-Mariposa KOA Kampground.** On Highway 140, 7 miles north of Mariposa. Has groceries, showers, laundromat, swimming pool. Open all year. Privately run.

3. **Denver Church Campground.** At Bass Lake. Has flush toilets, swimming. Open all year. Operated by California Land Management Company by agreement with the Forest Service.

4. **Forks Campground.** At Bass Lake. Has flush toilets, swimming. Open 5/1–10/31. Operated by California Land Management Company by agreement with the Forest Service.

5. **Lupine Campground.** At Bass Lake. Has flush toilets, swimming. Open 5/1–10/31. Operated by California Land Management Company by agreement with the Forest Service.

6. **Spring Cove Campground.** At Bass Lake. Has flush toilets, swimming. Open 5/1–9/30. Operated by California Land Management Company by agreement with the Forest Service.

7. **Wishon Point Campground.** At Bass Lake. Has flush toilets, swimming. Open 5/1–11/30. Operated by California Land Management Company by agreement with the Forest Service.

The gold rush-era courthouse in the town of Mariposa.

# Bass Lake
# to
# Shaver Lake

<u>39 miles</u> • Up Into the Woods Again

This section takes you from the relatively dry country around Bass Lake and North Fork down into a deep river valley, then 4,400 feet up to the heavily forested Shaver Lake area. This section is short because of the major climb involved, but strong, ambitious cyclists should be able to finish this and the next section to Camp 4½ in one day. But why push so hard that you will miss the scenery?

The main route between Shaver Lake and Highway 180 (Sections 4-6 and 4-7) contains several long stretches of unpaved or poorly-paved road through remote country. For those who would rather avoid such areas, Section 4-6 describes an all-paved, low-elevation shortcut from Highway 168 to Highway 180 via Pine Flat Reservoir and Piedra. That shortcut, approximately 20 miles shorter, departs from the main route in this section south of Auberry.

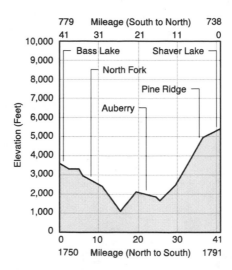

Just past Miller's Landing and Wishon Point Campground, leave Bass Lake on Road 222 (Crane Valley Road). Ride a little over 2 miles and make a left turn, continuing on Road 222 (now called Manzanita Road). Ride 0.8 mile and make a right turn, again continuing on Road 222 (Manzanita Road), heading south past Manzanita Lake. About 1 mile past the southern end of the lake is the town of North Fork which has stores and attracts tourists.

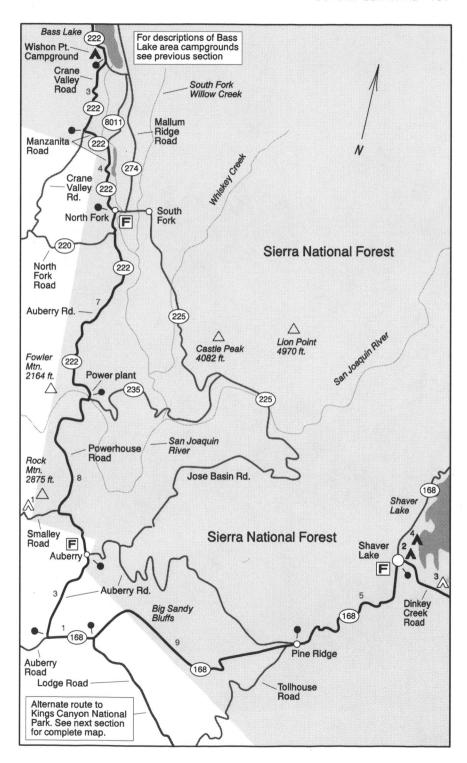

Cyclists near Mariposa on their way to Yosemite Park. Note the mix-and-match panniers.

From North Fork, head south on North Fork Road (still Road 222) for 1 mile until making a left turn onto Auberry Road (still Road 222). It is a long, steep, approximately 6-mile coast on Road 222 through dry countryside down to the San Joaquin River and Pacific Gas and Electric's Wishon Power House. Beyond that, the ride up Powerhouse Road can be sweaty, with the top of the grade reached 4 miles from the river. There are some worthwhile scenic outlooks along the way.

Three miles from the top of the grade is the town of Auberry with a supermarket. This is the logical place for a mid-day stop to replenish fluids and prepare for the long haul to Shaver Lake.

From Auberry it is possible to take Auberry Road east up toward Shaver Lake, but the gentler and very wide Highway 168 is the recommended route. From Auberry follow Auberry Road south for 3 miles before turning left onto Highway 168 and heading uphill for 10 miles to Pine Ridge.

*To take the shortcut between Highway 168 and Highway 180, turn off Highway 168 onto Lodge Road 2 miles east of the intersection of Auberry Road and Highway 168. The map, elevation profile and description for the shortcut are in the next section.*

After Pine Ridge (an elevation gain of 2,500 feet from Auberry), it is 5 miles and another 500 feet up to Shaver Lake on a now twisting and narrow Highway 168. Be careful as tractor-trailer rigs and logging trucks compete for the road.

Shaver Lake is a mountain tourist town with lots of stores and facilities. It is the last place to buy food on the main route until Grant Grove Village, 75 miles away (Section 4-7).

## Campgrounds

1. **Squaw Leap Campground.** 2 miles north of Auberry on Powerhouse Road, then 2 miles west on Smalley Road (a drop of 1,000 feet). Has no drinking water; groceries available in Auberry. Open all year. Bureau of Land Management.

2. **Dorabelle Campground.** 0.5 mile east of Shaver Lake off Highway 168 on Dorabelle Street. Has drinking water, swimming. Open 5/1–10/31. Forest Service.

3. **Swanson Campground.** On Dinkey Creek Road, 3 miles east of Shaver Lake. Has no drinking water. Open 5/1–11/30. Forest Service.

4. **Camp Edison.** On Highway 168, 1 mile northeast of Shaver Lake. Has showers, flush toilets, swimming. Open all year. Municipal park.

# Shaver Lake
# to
# Camp 4½

Includes an all-paved shortcut from Highway 168 to Highway 180.

48 miles • Backroads Solitude and Beauty

This section of the Trail involves some really away-from-it-all backcountry riding with miles of nary an automobile. Remember to stock up on food — Shaver Lake has the last food stores along the main route until Grant Grove Village in the next section.

From Shaver Lake there is a 1,700-foot climb to the beginning of unpaved Black Rock Road. Beyond is a relentless 6,000-foot drop through forested land and the magnificent canyon of the North Fork of the Kings River. Surprisingly, long downhills can be tiring too.

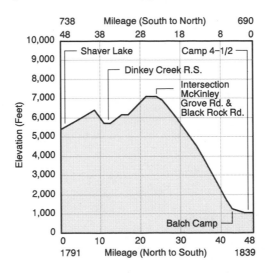

Just south of the town of Shaver Lake, take Dinkey Creek Road east from Highway 168 and ride 13 miles through forested areas to Dinkey Creek Ranger Station (water is available there). Here, turn right onto McKinley Grove Road, which is well-kept and paved. Five miles down the road is McKinley Grove with impressive, giant Sequoia trees and Gigantea Campground (#2).

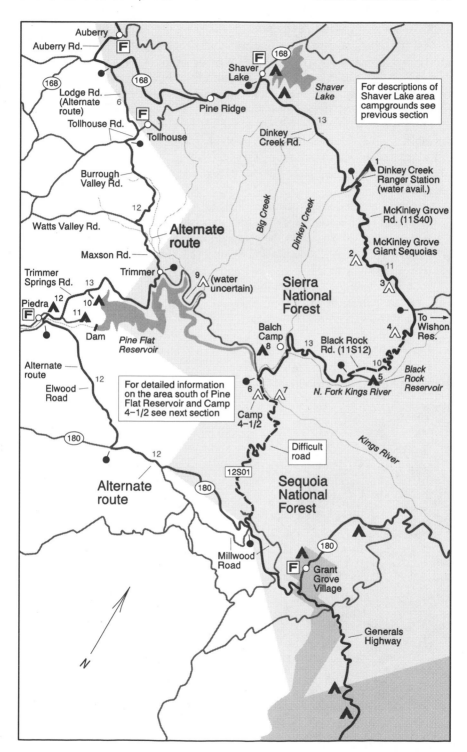

For descriptions of Shaver Lake area campgrounds see previous section

Auberry

Auberry Rd.

Lodge Rd. (Alternate route)

Tollhouse Rd.

Tollhouse

Pine Ridge

Shaver Lake

*Shaver Lake*

Dinkey Creek Rd.

Dinkey Creek Ranger Station (water avail.)

McKinley Grove Rd. (11S40)

McKinley Grove Giant Sequoias

Burrough Valley Rd.

Watts Valley Rd.

**Alternate route**

*Big Creek*

*Dinkey Creek*

Maxson Rd.

Trimmer

Trimmer Springs Rd.

Piedra

Dam

(water uncertain)

*Pine Flat Reservoir*

Balch Camp

Black Rock Rd. (11S12)

**Sierra National Forest**

To Wishon Res.

*Black Rock Reservoir*

*N. Fork Kings River*

Alternate route

Elwood Road

For detailed information on the area south of Pine Flat Reservoir and Camp 4-1/2 see next section

Camp 4-1/2

Difficult road

*Kings River*

**Alternate route**

12S01

**Sequoia National Forest**

Millwood Road

Grant Grove Village

Generals Highway

N

Six miles from McKinley Grove, and after passing Buck Meadow Campground (#3), turn right on semi-paved Black Rock Road (the paving is very spotty and unmaintained). The road may be marked by a sign indicating mileages to Sawmill Flat, Balch Camp, and Pine Flat Reservoir. The turnoff is about 300 yards before the Tule Meadows Trailer Park turnoff. If you pass over Long Meadow Creek on McKinley Grove Road you have gone too far.

From the turn onto Black Rock Road, the remainder of this section is all downhill. One mile down the unpaved road you will pass over the West Fork of Long Meadow Creek. The forest was humming with hovering yellow bees when I last went through — the kind that hang around picnic tables. A nuisance.

One mile beyond the West Fork of Long Meadow Creek is Sawmill Flat Campground (#4). After the campground, follow a sign that points to Black Rock Reservoir. Shortly after the campground all traces of pavement disappear and the dirt road is actually smoother. From this point on I only saw one vehicle all the way to Balch Camp.

Soon this road comes out on the edge of the gigantic canyon of the North Fork of the Kings River. Three miles later is a series of switchbacks; be careful not to lose control in the sandy spots. The coniferous forest gives way to maple trees; later, warm breaths of air from the valleys below replace the cool of the high elevations. After 9 miles of unpaved road, the paved road begins again near the turnoff for Black Rock Campground (#5). The campground, 1 mile away without much of a drop in elevation, has drinking water.

Black Rock Road in the canyon of the North Fork of the Kings River.

Now the road, edging downward, is cut into the rock of the steep canyon walls and passes under huge pipes carrying water from distant dams to a powerhouse below. The vistas on the descent through the canyon are spectacular. There are few guard rails on this road so be careful.

Ten miles from the turnoff for Black Rock Campground is Balch Camp, a small company town for power production personnel and their families. There is no store.

Three miles south of Balch Camp, just after crossing over the main branch of the Kings River (Rogers Crossing), turn left onto an unpaved road that follows the river and proceed about 1 mile to Camp 4½ (#6). Two other campgrounds are about a mile further down the road. None have piped drinking water although nearby river water can be purified.

The closest food store is in Piedra, some 30 miles to the west. If you intend to take the rigorous, unpaved road to Highway 180 described in the next section, you will need to be well-fed.

## Highway 168 to Highway 180 shortcut

This shortcut starts on Highway 168 in the previous section and intersects the main route on Highway 180 near Grant Grove Village. This shortcut is approximately 20 miles shorter than the main route and is all paved.

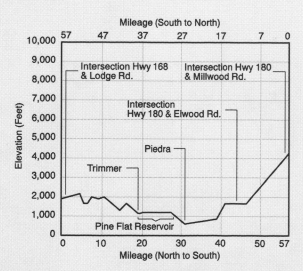

From Highway 168, 2 miles east of the intersection of Highway 168 and Auberry Road, turn right onto Lodge Road. You will encounter a series of small hills in the next 20 miles. Five miles from Highway 168 turn right onto Tollhouse Road. (If you are desperate for supplies, a left turn onto Tollhouse Road and a 1-mile ride will take you into Tollhouse, which has a store.)

Bike 1 mile on Tollhouse Road, then turn left onto Burrough Valley Road, then travel 4 miles to a left turn onto Maxson Road. Eight miles later you will arrive at the town of Trimmer and Pine Flat Reservoir. Trimmer has no stores.

In Trimmer, turn right and bike south, then west, on Trimmer Springs Road for 13 miles to Piedra, which has a cafe, post office, and store. In Piedra, make a left turn and bike 0.8 mile, crossing over the Kings River, before turning left onto Elwood Road. Follow it for 12 miles, gaining about 1,000 feet, to Highway 180.

Turn left onto Highway 180 and ride 12 miles, gaining about 2,500 feet, to the intersection of Highway 180 and Millwood Road.

*At the intersection of Highway 180 and Millwood Road, the short-cut joins the main route which emerges from the backcountry here. Continue east on Highway 180 as described in the middle of the next section.*

## Campgrounds

1. **Dinkey Creek Campground.** At end of Dinkey Creek Road. Has flush toilets, showers, swimming. Open 5/1–10/31. Forest Service.

2. **Gigantea Campground.** 6 miles southeast of Dinkey Creek Ranger Station on road to Wishon Reservoir. Has no drinking water. Open 6/1–10/31. Forest Service.

3. **Buck Meadow Campground.** 8 miles southeast of Dinkey Creek Ranger Station on road to Wishon Reservoir. Has no drinking water, but stream water can be purified; has swimming. Open 6/1–10/31. Forest Service.

   **Lily Pad Campground.** (not shown on map) 17 miles southeast of Dinkey Creek Ranger Station at Wishon Reservoir. Has drinking water, swimming. Open 6/1–10/31. Forest Service.

4. **Sawmill Flat Campground.** On road to Balch Camp, 3 miles south of road to Wishon Reservoir. Has no drinking water, but often has stream water which can be purified. Open 6/1–10/31. Forest Service.

5. **Black Rock Campground.** Off road to Balch Camp, 10 miles south of road to Wishon Reservoir. Has drinking water. Open 5/1–11/31. Forest Service.

6. **Camp 4½.** 3 miles south of Balch Camp on Trimmer Springs Road, then 0.6 mile southeast on unpaved road. Has no drinking water, but water from nearby Kings River can be purified. Open all year. Forest Service.

7. **Camp 4 and Mill Flat campgrounds.** About 1 mile and 2 miles east, respectively, of campground #6 on same unpaved road. Has no drinking water, but water from nearby Kings River can be purified. Open all year. Forest Service.

8. **Kirch Flat Campground.** 17 miles east of Trimmer on Trimmer Springs Road. Has drinking water, swimming. Open all year. Forest Service.

9. **Sycamore Flat campgrounds 1 and 2.** Both about 5 miles east of Trimmer on Trimmer Springs Road. Check in Trimmer to ensure campgrounds have water. Open all year. Forest Service.

10. **Island Park Campground.** 6 miles south of Trimmer on Trimmer Springs Road, then about 2 miles off on a side road. Has flush toilets. Open all year. Army Corps of Engineers.

11. **Pine Flat Recreation Area Campground.** 3 miles east of Piedra, off Trimmer Springs Road on a side road leading to Pine Flat Dam. Has flush toilets, nearby store in Piedra. Open all year. County park.

12. **Choinumni Park Campground.** On Trimmer Springs Road, 1 mile east of Piedra. Has drinking water, nearby store in Piedra. Open all year. County park.

Fishing the Kings River near Camp 4½.

# Camp 4½
# to
# Three Rivers

*Includes an optional side trip into Kings Canyon.*

<u>78 miles</u>  •  The Toughest Section

One look at this section's elevation profile says it all — there is little relief as you climb 6,500 feet.

The 18-mile mostly-unpaved main route between Camp 4½ and Highway 180 is the toughest part; you gain 3,100 feet on the unpaved road alone. Low elevation heat combined with the possibility of aggressive flies can make the going difficult. Some parts of the unpaved road have loose rock that require nimble cycling and there are some switchbacks. However, I did manage to bike the unpaved road with a non-mountain bike using 1¼ inch clincher tires with thick tubes. Get a very early start and take much more water than you think you will need.

After reaching Highway 180, there is another 2,400 feet of climbing to the level of Grant Grove Village, and another 900 feet to the highest point of this section. You're ironman material if you finish this section in one day carrying touring gear!

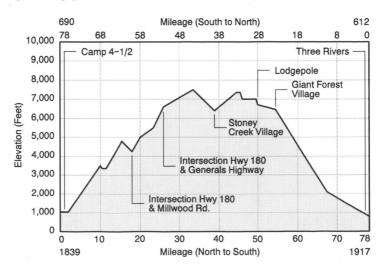

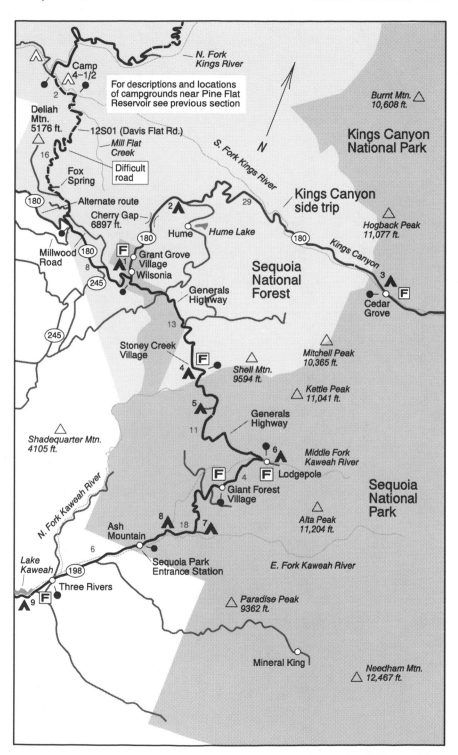

For descriptions and locations of campgrounds near Pine Flat Reservoir see previous section

N. Fork Kings River

Camp 4-1/2

2

Deliah Mtn. 5176 ft.

12S01 (Davis Flat Rd.)

Mill Flat Creek

16

Fox Spring

Difficult road

180

Alternate route

Cherry Gap 6897 ft.

2

180

Hume

Hume Lake

S. Fork Kings River

N

Kings Canyon National Park

Burnt Mtn. 10,608 ft.

Kings Canyon side trip

Hogback Peak 11,077 ft.

180

Kings Canyon

Millwood Road

180

8

245

F

Grant Grove Village

Wilsonia

Generals Highway

Sequoia National Forest

3

Cedar Grove

F

245

13

Stoney Creek Village

F

4

Shell Mtn. 9594 ft.

Mitchell Peak 10,365 ft.

Kettle Peak 11,041 ft.

5

11

Generals Highway

Shadequarter Mtn. 4105 ft.

6

Middle Fork Kaweah River

F

F

Lodgepole

Giant Forest Village

4

Sequoia National Park

N. Fork Kaweah River

8

18

7

Ash Mountain

Alta Peak 11,204 ft.

6

Lake Kaweah

198

Three Rivers

Sequoia Park Entrance Station

E. Fork Kaweah River

9

F

Paradise Peak 9362 ft.

Mineral King

Needham Mtn. 12,467 ft.

To begin this section, head further east on the road that you took to Camp 4¹/₂, passing Camp 4, and after 2 miles arrive at a turnoff marked by a sign announcing "Highway 180 — 16 miles." Turn right onto this road (Road 12S01 or Davis Flat Road). After 2 miles on Road 12S01 you will pass over a concrete spillway. There are cattle grazing free and a few houses in the area. The road then ascends through the picturesque valleys of Mill Flat Creek and Davis Creek. About 1 mile from the spillway you will pass a metal gate which blocks most vehicles from using the road beyond.

As the road winds upward, trees give way to brush and the hills are arid. Two miles from the metal gate is a small stream, but cattle walk through it. About 3 miles later the road levels off at Sampson Flat — there is even a little downhill riding. Then it is up again. About 2 miles after the resumption of the uphill is the turnoff for Fox Spring, 0.5 mile away. I have been told that the spring is active. One mile beyond the Fox Spring turnoff do not take the Deliah Lookout road. Finally, 1 mile beyond, the dirt road intersects a paved road.

Turn left onto the paved road (a right turn goes to a boy's camp), bike a short distance downhill, then turn right and coast about a mile down Mill-wood Road to Highway 180.

*The paved shortcut described in the previous section connects with the main route at this point.*

From the intersection of Millwood Road and Highway 180, it is a 2,300-foot climb to Grant Grove Village through increasingly lush forest; there is a gas station along the way with water. Watch for speeding logging trucks along this narrow, curvey highway. Six miles from the intersection is the Kings Canyon National Park entrance station where you will receive detailed information about the park. About 2 miles beyond you will reach the intersection of Highway 180 and Generals Highway.

From the intersection of Highway 180 and Generals Highway, the Grant Grove area of Kings Canyon Park is about 1 mile off the main route on Highway 180. It has three camping areas, and Wilsonia and Grant Grove Village have stores, restaurants, and lodging.

## Kings Canyon side trip

From Grant Grove Village it is possible to make a side trip on Highway 180 into Kings Canyon. The end of the road is 34 miles away. There are stores at Cedar Grove Village and campgrounds in the canyon. The map and the following elevation profile show the road into the canyon.

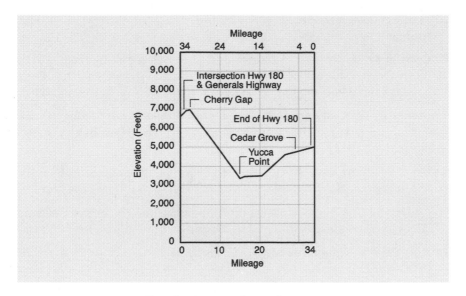

## Continuing on the main route

To continue to Three Rivers from the intersection of Highway 180 and Generals Highway, head southeast on Generals Highway, which carries considerable traffic. Twelve miles from the intersection, after a 1,000-foot rise and fall, is Stoney Creek Village with stores and a restaurant. Shortly afterwards you enter Sequoia National Park. Four miles beyond the national park boundary is Little Baldy Saddle cresting at 7,335 feet.

Six miles beyond Little Baldy is the Lodgepole visitor center along with a food store, post office, and campground. Four miles beyond (and larger than Lodgepole) is Giant Forest Village with restaurants, stores, and lodging. The forest in these areas is rich, with some spectacularly huge trees.

From Giant Forest Village the Trail begins a long descent on switchbacks through increasingly arid countryside as temperatures increase. The views are impressive.

Eighteen miles from Giant Forest Village is the Ash Mountain entrance station to Sequoia National Park and the park headquarters. Six miles beyond is the city of Three Rivers with stores, motels, and restaurants at an elevation of 800 feet. If you have come all the way from Camp 4½ you deserve a cool shower or swim.

## Campgrounds

1. **Azalea, Crystal Springs, and Sunset campgrounds.** All near Grant Grove Village and Wilsonia. All have showers and flush toilets. Azalea is open all year; others close for various periods. National Park Service.

2. **Princess Campground.** On Highway 180, 6 miles north of Wilsonia. Has flush toilets. Open 5/1–10/31. Forest Service.

3. **Canyon View, Moraine, Sentinel, and Sheep Creek campgrounds.** On Kings Canyon side trip near Cedar Grove Village. All have showers, flush toilets. At least one campground is open 4/1–10/31. National Park Service.

4. **Stoney Creek Campground.** On Generals Highway near Stoney Creek Village, 13 miles southeast of Grant Grove Village. Has drinking water. Open 6/1–10/31. Forest Service.

5. **Dorst Campground.** Off Generals Highway, 5 miles southeast of Stoney Creek Village. Has flush toilets. Open 6/15–9/10. National Park Service.

6. **Lodgepole Campground.** Near Lodgepole visitor center on Generals Highway. Has showers, flush toilets. Open all year. National Park Service.

7. **Buckeye Flat Campground.** Off Generals Highway, 10 miles south of Giant Forest Village. Has flush toilets. Open 4/10–11/1. National Park Service.

8. **Potwisha Campground.** Off Generals Highway, 3 miles north of Sequoia National Park entrance station at Ash Mountain. Has flush toilets. Open all year. National Park Service.

9. **Horse Creek Recreation Area Campground.** On Highway 198 at Lake Kaweah, 6 miles southwest of Three Rivers. Has flush toilets. Open all year. Army Corps of Engineers.

A giant Sequoia tree along Generals Highway.

# Three Rivers
# to
# Camp Nelson

<u>59 miles</u>  •  Warm Sierra Foothills

In the summer you should get an early start to avoid the heat of the low-elevation foothills that make up most of this section. The final 15 miles follow the canyon of the Middle Fork of the Tule River through forests to an elevation of nearly 5,000 feet.

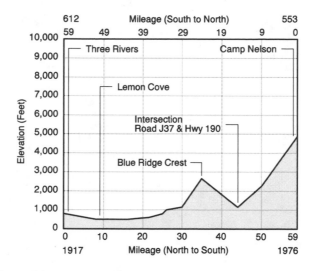

From Three Rivers take Highway 198 southwest for 9 miles to Lemoncove, which has stores and a nearby KOA campground (#1). Seven miles southwest of Lemoncove turn left onto Yokohl Drive, also known as Mountain Road 296, and head southeast amid dry, grassy hills and lots of ground squirrels. The road gradually rises, getting steeper as switchbacks begin at Blue Ridge (a "ridge," not a town). Nineteen miles from the Yokohl Drive turnoff you reach the 2,600-foot crest of the ridge.

Ride 3 miles downhill and east to the junction with Road J37. Continue south on Road J37 another 6 miles to its intersection with Highway 190 at the outskirts of Springville. To enter Springville, which has a store, turn right onto Highway 190.

To continue on the Trail turn left onto Highway 190 and start climbing up a valley alongside the rushing waters of the Middle Fork of the Tule River. Some portions of Highway 190 are steep and there can be considerable traffic. Nine miles up from Springville is a Pacific Gas and Electric hydroelectric

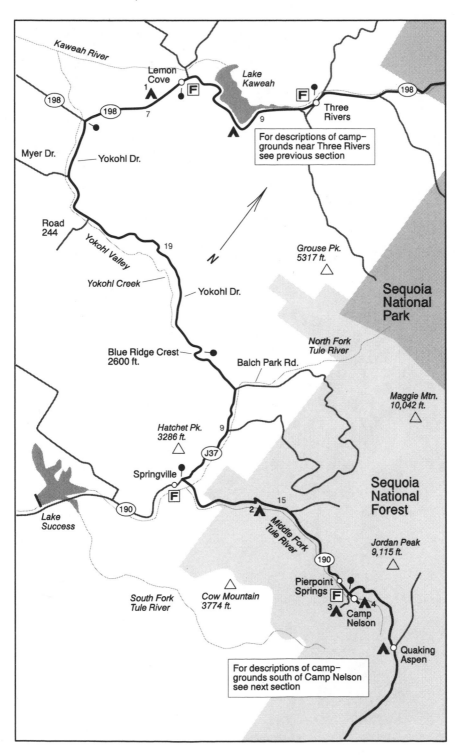

For descriptions of camp-grounds near Three Rivers see previous section

For descriptions of camp-grounds south of Camp Nelson see next section

Highway 190 on the way to Camp Nelson.

power station. Five miles beyond is Pierpoint Springs Resort with a grocery store and restaurant. This is a good place to buy food if you will be staying in the Camp Nelson area.

One mile later, at 4,800 feet, is Camp Nelson, with two restaurants and a store. The two campgrounds in the area are situated in dense, scenic forests.

## Campgrounds

1. **Lemoncove-Sequoia KOA.** On Highway 198, 1 mile southwest of Lemoncove. Has flush toilets, showers, swimming. Open all year. Privately run.

2. **Coffee Camp Campground.** On Highway 190, 5 miles east of Springville. Has drinking water, swimming. Open all year. Forest Service.

3. **Coy Flat Campground.** 0.5 mile south of Camp Nelson. Has drinking water, swimming. Open 3/15–9/30. Forest Service.

4. **Belknap Campground.** 2 miles east of Camp Nelson. Has drinking water. Open 3/15–9/30. Forest Service.

# Camp Nelson
# to
# Wofford Heights

<u>57 miles</u>  •  Beautiful Cycling

This is one of the easy ones — after climbing 2,000 feet and crossing a few hills, enjoy a long downhill ride through the Kern River Canyon to Lake Isabella. There are many campgrounds along this stretch of the Trail.

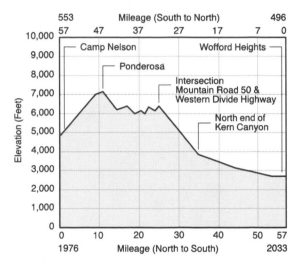

If you stayed at Belknap Campground, there is a shortcut back up to Highway 190 if you are headed toward Lake Isabella. Head back toward Highway 190 on the same road that brought you to the campground, but just past the Camp Nelson store turn right onto Smith Drive. Go one block, then turn left onto Sutherland Drive, which leads up to Highway 190. Turn right onto Highway 190.

Proceed uphill on Highway 190. Six miles away is Cedar Slope with a restaurant and a store, which are only open during the summer. Four miles from Cedar Slope, at Quaking Aspen, Highway 190 ends and the Western Divide Highway begins. Two miles beyond is a place called Ponderosa with a small store and restaurant. This is the last chance to buy food before Kernville. Ponderosa also marks this section's high point at about 7,200 feet.

Cross three hills over the next 14 miles before reaching the turnoff for Mountain Road 50 at the top of a fourth hill. Turn left here and bike east on Western Divide Highway (also known as Mountain Road 99).

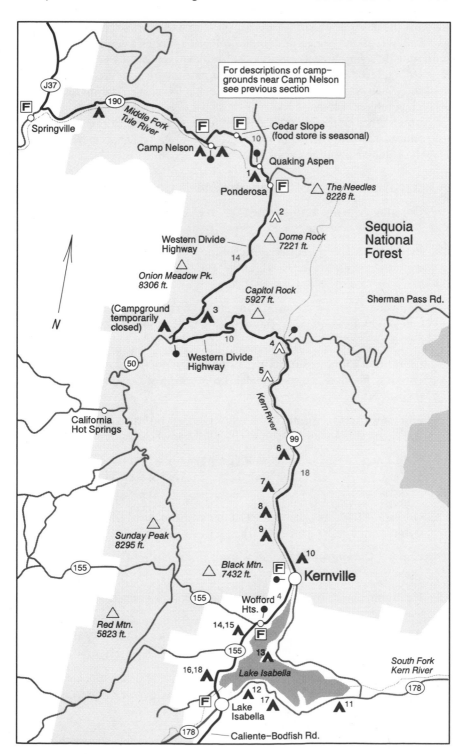

For descriptions of camp-
grounds near Camp Nelson
see previous section

J37

F
Springville

190

Middle Fork
Tule River

Camp Nelson

F

F
10

Cedar Slope
(food store is seasonal)

Quaking Aspen

1

Ponderosa

F

The Needles
8228 ft.

2

Dome Rock
7221 ft.

Western Divide
Highway

14

Sequoia
National
Forest

Onion Meadow Pk.
8306 ft.

Capitol Rock
5927 ft.

Sherman Pass Rd.

N

(Campground
temporarily
closed)

3

50

Western Divide
Highway

10

4

5

Kern River

California
Hot Springs

99

6

18

7

8

9

Sunday Peak
8295 ft.

10

155

Black Mtn.
7432 ft.

F

Kernville

Wofford 4
Hts.

F

Red Mtn.
5823 ft.

155

14,15

F

155

13

16,18

Lake Isabella

South Fork
Kern River

178

12

F

17

11

Lake
Isabella

178

Caliente–Bodfish Rd.

Now the day's downhill riding begins. From the junction with Mountain Road 50, it is 10 miles east on Mountain Road 99 to the beautiful Kern River with its wild river currents, rafters, and red canyon walls. Follow Mountain Road 99 eighteen miles down the canyon past many campgrounds to Kernville and Lake Isabella. As one gets lower and lower, vegetation diminishes and temperatures increase.

Kernville has stores, motels, and restaurants. The end of this section is 4 miles ahead at Wofford Heights on Highway 155. As you can see below, Lake Isabella is blessed with many campgrounds.

## Campgrounds

1. **Quaking Aspen Campground.** On Highway 190, 9 miles east of Camp Nelson. Has drinking water. Open 5/1–10/31. Forest Service.

2. **Peppermint Campground.** Approximately 1 mile south of Ponderosa, then a short distance off Highway 190. Has no drinking water. Open 5/25–10/15. Forest Service.

3. **Redwood Meadow Campground.** Off Western Divide Highway, 10 miles south of Ponderosa. Has drinking water. Open 5/25–10/15. Forest Service.

4. **Limestone Campground.** First campground upon reaching Kern River; 18 miles north of Kernville. Has no drinking water. Open 5/15–10/1. Forest Service.

5. **Fairview Campground.** On Kern River, 16 miles north of Kernville. Has no drinking water. Open 5/15–10/1. Forest Service.

6. **Gold Ledge and Corral Creek campgrounds.** On Kern River, 10 miles north of Kernville. Both have drinking water. Open 5/15–10/1. Forest Service.

7. **Hospital Flat Campground.** 6 miles north of Kernville. Has drinking water, swimming. Open 5/15–10/1. Forest Service.

8. **Camp 3 Campground.** 5 miles north of Kernville. Has drinking water. Open 5/15–10/1. Forest Service.

9. **Headquarters Campground.** 4 miles north of Kernville. Has drinking water. Open all year. Forest Service.

10. **Rivernook Campground.** 0.5 mile north of Kernville at 14001 Sierra Way. Has flush toilets, showers. Open all year. Privately run.

11. **KOA Lake Isabella.** On Highway 178, 10 miles east of city of Lake Isabella. Has flush toilets, showers, swimming. Open all year. Privately run.

*The following campgrounds are run by the Army Corps of Engineers near Lake Isabella. During the summer months they are often full. They all have drinking water and swimming.*

12. **Auxiliary Dam Campground.** On Highway 178, 1 mile north of city of Lake Isabella. Has flush toilets, showers. Open all year.

13. **Eastside Campground.** 5 miles south of Kernville on east side of Lake Isabella. Has flush toilets. Open all year.

14. **Live Oak Campground.** Off Highway 155, 0.5 mile south of Wofford Heights. Has flush toilets, showers. Open 4/1–9/31.

15. **Tillie Creek Campground.** Off Highway 155, 1 mile south of Wofford Heights. Has flush toilets, showers. Open all year.

16. **Main Dam Campground.** On Highway 155, 1 mile northwest of city of Lake Isabella. Has flush toilets. Open 4/1–9/31.

17. **Paradise Cove Campground.** On Highway 178, 6 miles east of city of Lake Isabella. Has flush toilets. Open all year.

18. **Pioneer Point Campground.** On Highway 155, 2 miles northwest of city of Lake Isabella. Has flush toilets, showers. Open all year.

The untamed Kern River in its upper reaches along Mountain Road 99.

# Wofford Heights
# to
# Tehachapi

60 miles • The Southern, Southern, Southern Sierra Nevada

This section, the last in the Sierra Nevada, takes the Trail over three ridges, up onto a dry plateau, then down a lonely canyon to tiny Caliente ("hot" in Spanish), which often lives up to its name. Then it is up 2,700 feet into Tehachapi Pass and finally the city of Tehachapi. After the Lake Isabella area there are no campgrounds with drinking water until Tehachapi.

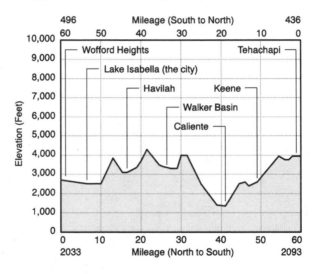

From Wofford Heights, head south 7 miles on Highway 155 to the city of Lake Isabella at the south end of the reservoir. As you approach the city, cross over Highway 178, then turn right onto Lake Isabella Blvd., and head south to the town of Bodfish, which has a strip of stores. In Bodfish, bear left onto Caliente-Bodfish Road and continue south.

Begin rigorously climbing up Bodfish Grade on switchbacks. Three miles from Bodfish, the "bodacious" climb ends at the 3,800-foot crest. After three more miles you bottom out at the historic-looking town of Havilah. The countryside is dry. Beyond Havilah, be prepared for increasingly steep uphill work. Five miles from Havilah is the second crest at 4,300 feet. In the past there has been a general store at the crest called Piute Meadows Trading Post.

Then it is down again; the bottom of the grade is reached after 3 miles. After 1 mile on the often breezy Walker Basin, turn right (do not turn left toward Paris-Loraine).

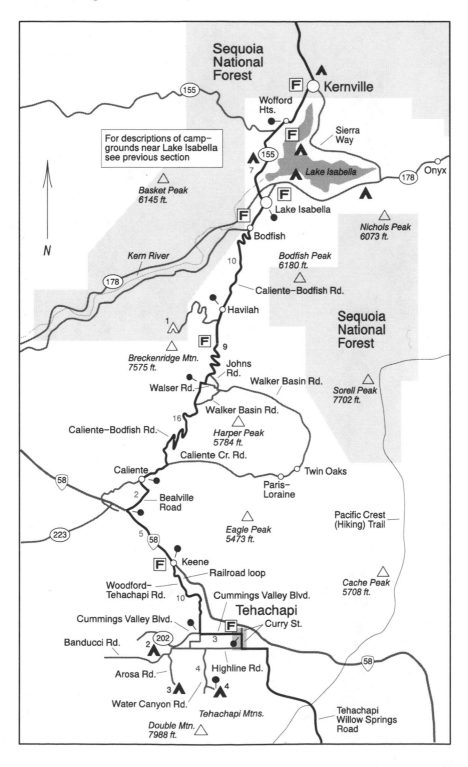

Sequoia
National
Forest

155

Wofford
Hts.

F  Kernville

F

Sierra
Way

155

7

Lake Isabella

178

Onyx

For descriptions of camp-
grounds near Lake Isabella
see previous section

Basket Peak
6145 ft.

F

F  Lake Isabella

Nichols Peak
6073 ft.

N

Kern River

F  Bodfish

10

Bodfish Peak
6180 ft.

Sequoia
National
Forest

178

Caliente–Bodfish Rd.

Havilah

1

F  9

Breckenridge Mtn.
7575 ft.

Johns
Rd.

Walker Basin Rd.

Sorell Peak
7702 ft.

Walser Rd.

Caliente–Bodfish Rd.

16

Walker Basin Rd.

Harper Peak
5784 ft.

Caliente Cr. Rd.

58

Caliente

2

Bealville
Road

Twin Oaks

Paris–
Loraine

223

5  58

Eagle Peak
5473 ft.

Pacific Crest
(Hiking) Trail

F  Keene

Railroad loop

Cache Peak
5708 ft.

Woodford–
Tehachapi Rd.

10

Cummings Valley Blvd.

Tehachapi

Cummings Valley Blvd.

F  Curry St.

Banducci Rd.

2  202

3

Arosa Rd.

4

Highline Rd.

58

Water Canyon Rd.

3

4

Double Mtn.
7988 ft.

Tehachapi Mtns.

Tehachapi
Willow Springs
Road

Bodfish-Caliente Road following the long, dry canyon before Caliente.

Three miles after the turn, begin another grade. This is getting repetitious! One mile later is the crest at 4,000 feet. Ride for 2 miles on a scenic plateau before beginning a 7-mile downhill ride through a dry canyon with switchbacks and a few starved-looking cattle. A few miles beyond is Caliente, with only a post office and railroad yards. You have dropped 2,700 feet from the plateau above.

At Caliente, leave Caliente-Bodfish Road and take Bealville Road south through a railroad underpass. Then climb 1,200 feet through 2 miles of grassy hills to Freeway 58. Turn left onto Freeway 58; it is legal to use heavily-travelled Freeway 58 for awhile because at this point it is the only road up into Tehachapi Pass. Still, an occasional driver will think you don't belong and honk; ride as far to the right as possible.

There is much train activity in this area because Tehachapi Pass is a major rail route through the southern Sierra Nevada. Later on, the bicycle route passes a spot where long trains circle over themselves to gain or lose elevation.

Nearly 5 miles after starting on Freeway 58, take the Keene exit (Keene has a store), go under the freeway, continue south along a road which parallels the freeway, then pass under it again as the road becomes Woodford-Tehachapi Road. This often-winding and ascending road has little traffic and is picturesque. Ten miles from Keene is the intersection of Woodford-Tehachapi Road and Cummings Valley Blvd. (Highway 202) on the outskirts of Tehachapi. The city, nestled in a depression between high hills, is nearly 4,000 feet high and can get quite cool and breezy.

To get to downtown Tehachapi, turn left onto Cummings Valley Blvd. and bike about 2 miles before making a left turn onto Curry Street and travelling 7 or 8 blocks. However, to continue on the main route south, turn right onto Curry Street. There are motels, restaurants, and stores in Tehachapi.

## Campgrounds

1. **Breckenridge Campground.** Turnoff is 2 miles south of Havilah on Bodfish-Caliente Road, then 8 miles and a 3,600-foot climb on an unpaved road. Has no drinking water. Open 5/1–10/31. Forest Service.

   *To get to the campgrounds near Tehachapi follow this common route: from the intersection of Woodford-Tehachapi Road and Cummings Valley Blvd. (Highway 202) proceed 0.5 mile further south on Woodford-Tehachapi Road, then turn right onto Schout Road and bike 0.5 mile west to a left turn onto Backes Lane. Bike 0.5 mile south on Backes Lane to the intersection of Backes Lane and Highline Road.*

2. **Brite Lake Recreation Area Campground.** At the intersection of Backes Lane and Highline Road turn right and bike 1 mile west on Highline Road. Continue on Banducci Road for 2 miles, arriving at Brite Valley Lake. The campground is on the west end of the lake. Has flush toilets. Open 5/1–10/31. Municipal park.

3. **Indian Hill Ranch Campground.** At the intersection of Backes Lane and Highline Road, turn right and bike 1 mile west on Highline Road. Continue on Banducci Road for 0.6 mile before making a left turn onto Arosa Road and biking 2 miles. Has showers. Open most of year. Privately run.

4. **Tehachapi Mountain Park Campground.** At the intersection of Backes Lane and Highline Road, turn left and bike 0.7 mile on Highline Road to a right turn onto Water Canyon Road. Campground is 3 miles away with a climb of 1,700 feet. Has drinking water. Open all year. County park.

# Region 5
# Southern California

A Joshua tree in Antelope Valley.

# Tehachapi
# to
# Monte Cristo Campground

## 72 miles • A Stretch of Desert

This first section of the Southern California portion of the Trail takes you out of the southern Sierra Nevada, across a portion of the Mojave Desert, and up into the San Gabriel Mountains north of Los Angeles. During the warmer months of the year, try to make the desert crossing early in the day.

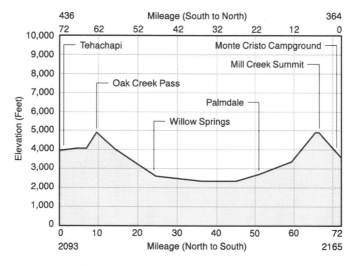

At the intersection of Woodford-Tehachapi Road and Cummings Valley Blvd. (Highway 202), turn left onto Cummings Valley Blvd., ride about 2 miles, turn right onto Curry Street, and ride about 1 mile to Highline Road. Turn left onto Highline Road and ride about 3 miles before turning right onto Tehachapi-Willow Springs Road. Three miles from the intersection of Highline Road and Tehachapi-Willow Springs Road you reach windy Oak Creek Pass, populated by hundreds of windmills of every variety imaginable. Some whirl away energetically, generating pollutionless electricity, while motionless companions seem to say — "Well, it isn't quite windy enough for me to bother."

After the windmill farm there is a long, gradual 15-mile downhill which ends at a small store at Willow Springs. Now the Trail has entered true desert country with a dramatic change in flora from all previous portions of the Trail. You can feel quite lonely out in these open spaces.

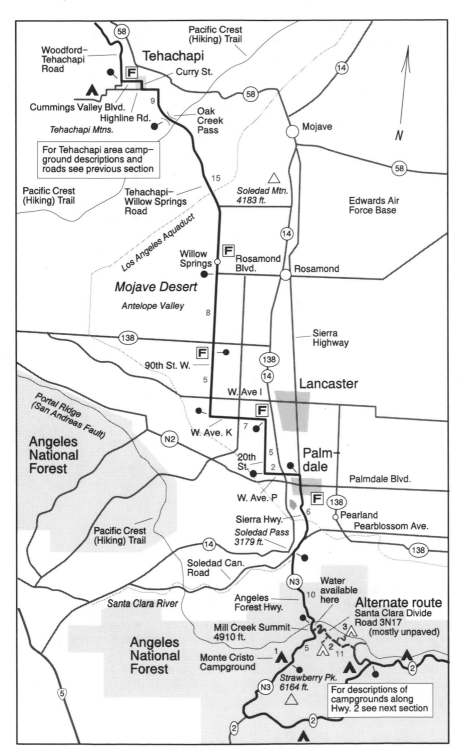

Pacific Crest (Hiking) Trail

58

Woodford–Tehachapi Road

Tehachapi

Curry St.

F

14

Cummings Valley Blvd.

Highline Rd.

*Tehachapi Mtns.*

9

58

Oak Creek Pass

Mojave

N

For Tehachapi area camp-ground descriptions and roads see previous section

Pacific Crest (Hiking) Trail

Tehachapi–Willow Springs Road

15

*Soledad Mtn. 4183 ft.*

58

Edwards Air Force Base

*Los Angeles Aquaduct*

Willow Springs

F

Rosamond Blvd.

14

Rosamond

*Mojave Desert*

*Antelope Valley*

8

Sierra Highway

138

F

90th St. W.

5

138

14

W. Ave I

Lancaster

*Portal Ridge (San Andreas Fault)*

Angeles National Forest

N2

W. Ave. K

F

7

20th St.

5

2

Palm-dale

Palmdale Blvd.

Pacific Crest (Hiking) Trail

14

W. Ave. P

F

138

Pearland

Pearblossom Ave.

Sierra Hwy.

*Soledad Pass 3179 ft.*

6

138

Soledad Can. Road

*Santa Clara River*

N3

Angeles Forest Hwy.

10

Water available here

Alternate route

Santa Clara Divide Road 3N17 (mostly unpaved)

Mill Creek Summit 4910 ft.

3

Angeles National Forest

Monte Cristo Campground

1

5

2

11

N3

*Strawberry Pk. 6164 ft.*

For descriptions of campgrounds along Hwy. 2 see next section

2

5

2

2

Continue heading south on Tehachapi-Willow Springs Road, which becomes 90th Street West. Straight ahead to the south is Portal Ridge, marking the San Andreas earthquake fault. Eight miles beyond the store at Willow Springs is a second, larger one. Five miles later, turn left onto West Avenue K.

Proceed about 7 miles on West Avenue K and enter the outskirts of Lancaster. You may well wonder how such a prosperous-looking community might exist in such a hot-summer locale. One answer is the aircraft plants in the area. Also, only a few miles away is the Edwards Air Force Base landing site for the space shuttle.

Turn right onto 20th Street (there is a grocery store on this corner) and ride south about 5 miles before making a left turn onto West Avenue P. Bike 2 miles east on West Avenue P before turning right onto Sierra Highway and rolling into Palmdale — another large, bustling city on the desert's edge with all manner of stores, motels, etc. You may wish to stock up with food here.

Continue south on Sierra Highway. When Pearblossom Highway joins this road, you will encounter considerable traffic. After riding through an underpass about 5 miles south of Palmdale, turn left and take the Angeles Forest Highway (Highway N3). A sign here says the Angeles Crest Highway is 25 miles away. Soon the road heads upward amid arid, sparsely-forested mountains. In the spring, there often are amazingly beautiful clusters of flowers and plants along the roadside.

Ten miles from the turnoff onto Highway N3 is Mill Creek Summit at 4,910 feet. Here you will find a small picnic area with water, a toilet, and another crossing of the Pacific Crest (Hiking) Trail. Maybe some day the hiking trail will have signs that announce the crossing of the bicycle trail! There is also a ranger station here.

*At Mill Creek Summit you must make a decision. For the more adventurous, there is the 11-mile, mostly unpaved Santa Clara Divide Road shortcut to the Angeles Crest Highway. It roughly follows the Pacific Crest (Hiking) Trail.*

### Santa Clara Divide Road shortcut

The dirt-and-sand road shortcut begins next to the Ranger Station at Mill Creek Summit and is designated "Santa Clara Divide Road 3N17." The shortcut has 8 miles of dirt and sand road, and 3 miles of paved road. The first mile or so is all uphill and frequent sandy spots forced me to walk my bike much of the way. Five miles from the ranger station the downhill begins. If you like isolation, you will find it on this road.

Halfway along the dirt road portion there are side roads leading to several campgrounds (without water), and there are several more (with water) near Angeles Crest Highway on the far end of this shortcut (see next section).

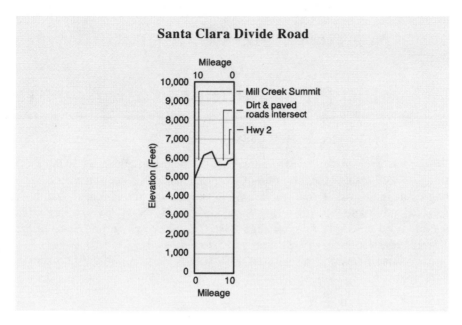

**Santa Clara Divide Road**

## Continuing on the main route

The all-paved main route is 27 miles longer and has 1,000 feet more climbing than the shortcut route. Nevertheless, the travel times may be equivalent considering the slowness of cycling on a dirt and sand road.

From Mill Creek Summit, continue on the main route by descending 5 miles on paved Highway N3 to Monte Cristo Campground (#1). There is a store 3 miles further south on Highway N3.

## Campgrounds

1. **Monte Cristo Campground.** On Highway N3, 5 miles south of Mill Creek Summit. Has drinking water, swimming. Open all year. Forest Service.

   *The following campgrounds are off the dirt-and-sand road shortcut. For campgrounds at the end of the shortcut, where it meets the Angeles Crest Highway, see the next section.*

2. **Roundtop Ridge Campground.** From Highway N3, about 3 miles southeast on Santa Clara Divide Road (3N17), it is about 2 miles on a side road to the campground. Has no drinking water. Open 4/1–10/31. Forest Service.

3. **Mt. Pacifico Campground.** From Highway N3, about 5 miles southeast on Santa Clara Divide Road (3N17), it is about 1 mile on a side road with a climb to the campground. Has no drinking water. Open 4/1–9/30. Forest Service.

# Monte Cristo Campground
# to
# Big Pines Ranger Station

55 miles • A Good Road and Great Mountains

Who would ever think that one of the more scenic mountain roads on the Trail lies just north of the megalopolis of Los Angeles? This section of the Trail begins in semi-arid, rather barren hills, and climbs into higher, dramatic, forested mountains by way of the Angeles Crest Highway. Even though this section is on the short side, mileage-wise, the many ups and downs and the overall elevation gain will burn up a lot of energy.

You should expect considerable traffic on weekends and holidays on the Angeles Crest Highway.

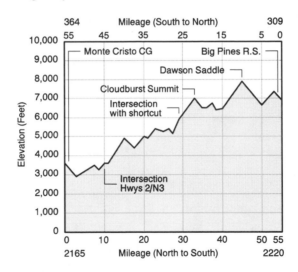

Leave Monte Cristo Campground and head south and downhill on Highway N3. There is a store 3 miles beyond the campground which is the last store until the end of this section. Just after the store, pass through a tunnel and cross a bridge to the other side of the canyon. Three miles from the store you will intersect Big Tujunga Canyon Road; stay left and remain on Highway N3. After the intersection, the road climbs for 4 miles until meeting Angeles Crest Highway, also known as Highway 2. Turn left onto Highway 2 and head east.

The terrain is still semi-arid. Ride for about a mile before heading up again. About 4 miles from the intersection of Highway N3 and Highway 2, you will reach the turnoff for Valley Forge Campground (#1). From the

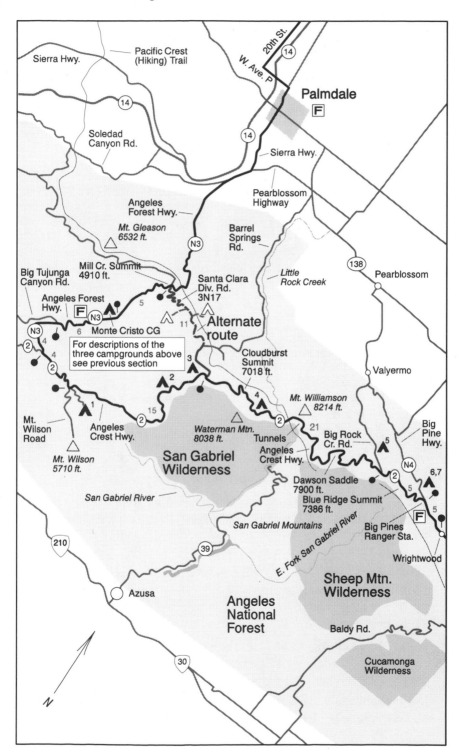

turnoff for Valley Forge Campground, climb to 5,400 feet in 11 miles to the turnoff for Chilao Campground (#2). Four miles beyond that is the intersection with the mostly unpaved Santa Clara Divide Road shortcut described in the previous section. Here, Horse Flats and Bandido Group campgrounds (#3) are several miles off Highway 2 on a paved road.

*The shortcut started in the previous section intersects the main route here.*

Proceed to climb another 1,100 feet over 4 miles to Cloudburst Summit (elevation 7,000 feet). A mile later and downhill is Buckhorn Campground (#4). Continuing (and after passing the Kratka Ridge Ski Area) you reach three picnic grounds in quick succession: Vista, Ridgecrest, and Eagles Roost. Signs say no camping. In this area, the Pacific Crest (Hiking) Trail lies close to the highway.

Prepare to pass through several short tunnels; the echoes are wonderful if there is no traffic to interfere. It is on this part of the highway that the mountain scenery becomes spectacular, with steep mountain slopes and deep valleys.

After the tunnels, again climb (past a spring) for 7 miles until you reach Dawson Saddle — which at 7,900 feet is the high point of this section.

Then there are 5 miles of downhill, followed by a 3-mile climb and a 2-mile descent to the intersection of Highway 2 and Highway N4. Big Pines Ranger Station and an outside telephone are located here. Three campgrounds are located several miles away on Highway N4. One mile toward Wrightwood on Highway 2 is a large food store.

I think you will agree that bicycling the Angeles Crest Highway is a memorable experience.

### Campgrounds

1. **Valley Forge Campground.** Turnoff, situated on Highway 2, is 4 miles east of the intersection of Highway N3 and Highway 2, and adjacent to turnoff for Mt. Wilson Observatory. Campground is 4 miles from Highway 2 on unpaved road. Has drinking water, swimming. Open 4/1–11/31. Forest Service.

2. **Chilao Campground.** On Highway 2, 13 miles northeast of intersection of Highway N3 and Highway 2. Has drinking water. Open 5/1–11/31. Forest Service.

3. **Horse Flats and Bandido Group campgrounds.** Several miles from Highway 2 on Santa Clara Divide Road (3N17, the shortcut). Both have drinking water. Open 5/1–11/31. Forest Service.

4. **Buckhorn Campground.** On Highway 2 about 23 miles west of Big Pines Ranger Station. Has drinking water. Open 5/1–10/31. Forest Service.

5. **Big Rock Campground.** About 4 miles west of Big Pines Ranger Station on Highway 2, then 2 miles northwest on Big Rock Creek Road. Has drinking water. Open 6/1–10/31. Forest Service.

6. **Peavine and Apple Tree campgrounds.** Both about 2 miles northwest of Big Pines Ranger Station on Highway N4. Both have drinking water. Open 5/1–11/30. Forest Service.

7. **Mountain Oak Campground.** On Highway N4, 0.5 mile beyond campground #6. Has flush toilets. Open 5/1–10/31. Forest Service.

Looking south from the Angeles Crest Highway near Dawson Saddle.

# Big Pines Ranger Station
# to
# Big Bear Lake

67 miles • To Mountain Resorts

After a 15-mile downhill through increasingly dry country, the Trail leaves the San Gabriel Mountains and crosses Cajon Junction before climbing past three resort-area lakes in the San Bernardino Mountains. The lake country has many small cities and stores. Be aware that traffic on the major roads can be heavy on holidays and weekends.

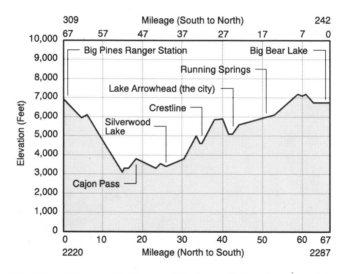

From Big Pines Ranger Station on Highway 2, head east and downhill on Highway 2 for 1 mile to a large store. Soon the trendy city of Wrightwood with plenty of stores and motels begins. Within the residential area of Wrightwood do not take the signed turnoff for Lone Pine Canyon from Highway 2 — it dead-ends! Rather, bike several blocks further and take a right turn onto Sheep Creek Road. After about 0.5 mile, turn left onto Lone Pine Canyon Road and head east. Sloping gradually downhill as it follows the San Andreas Fault, Lone Pine Canyon is quite picturesque with many towering yucca plants and hardly a car to be seen or heard. This is a paved 10-mile shortcut to Highway 138 and Cajon Pass.

Turn right upon reaching Highway 138, which carries considerable traffic, and proceed about a mile to the Freeway 15 overpass. There are gas stations and convenience stores here. Called Cajon Junction, this is the low-elevation

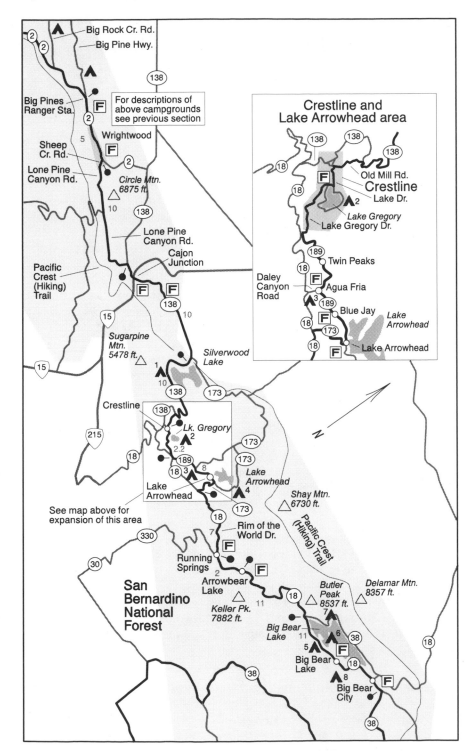

spot of the day at 3,100 feet. Immediately past Cajon Junction, begin climbing on Highway 138, until 3 miles from Cajon Junction you reach the summit of Cajon Pass at 3,800 feet. Now there is a 5-mile downhill ride to Silverwood Lake, which has a campground (#1). Widely separated between the pass and the lake are a store and a restaurant.

Two miles after leaving Silverwood Lake, the day's real climbing (steep at times) begins on Highway 138 with a 1,600-foot, 7-mile climb. Before reaching the crest on Highway 138, turn left onto Old Mill Road and continue climbing. This area is beautifully wooded and often cool. Just after the crest on Old Mill Road (1 mile from Highway 138) is a short, steep downhill into the town of Crestline. At the bottom, turn left onto Lake Drive and ride a short distance into Lake Gregory Village, full of stores, restaurants, and tourists.

Near the lake in Lake Gregory Village, turn right onto Lake Gregory Drive and bike 2 miles up a narrow, smooth road to a left turn onto Highway 189. The turnoff is just before an intersection with Highway 18 (Rim of the World Drive). Then there are 2 miles of fairly steep climbing to the town of Twin Peaks. After another 2 miles is the town of Agua Fria which has stores and restaurants. Dogwood Campground (#3) is 1 mile away off Daley Canyon Road. Less than a mile beyond Agua Fria (still on Highway 189) and downhill is the town of Blue Jay with stores. These areas are all forested.

Just ahead, follow the shoreline of Lake Arrowhead for a mile before turning right onto Highway 173 and heading uphill. Two miles later, turn left onto Highway 18 (Rim of the World Drive). Highway 18 can be very busy with traffic during commute times, on weekends, and on holidays.

Los Angeles basin smog occasionally reaches up this far. However, on smog-free days you will be able to see down into San Bernardino and Redlands some 5,000 feet below.

Seven miles up from the intersection of Highway 173 and Highway 18 is the town of Running Springs with stores and motels. Two miles beyond on fairly level Highway 18 is the town of Arrowbear Lake with stores. With some up and down work, the Trail now gains 1,000 feet, passing a ski resort or two, and cresting 6 miles from Arrowbear Lake on a 2-mile-long plateau of sorts. After a 2-mile downhill, the Big Bear Lake dam suddenly comes into view. Remain on Highway 18; 3 miles after the dam is the turnoff for Coldbrook Campground (#5) in the city of Big Bear Lake.

This prosperous city has a bike shop, youth hostel, stores, restaurants, motels, and campgrounds, although many close during the off-tourist season. The Pacific Crest (Hiking) Trail lies 2 miles north of the lake. At this elevation (6,750 feet) nighttime temperatures can get downright cold.

## Campgrounds

1. **Silverwood Lake State Recreation Area (Mesa Campground).**  On Cleghorn Road, about 1 mile from Highway 138 at west end of Silverwood Lake. Has showers, flush toilets. Open all year. State of California.

2. **Camp Switzerland Campground.** On Lake Drive at north end of Lake Gregory. Has flush toilets, showers. Open all year. Privately run.

3. **Dogwood Campground.** Off Daley Canyon Road about 1 mile south of Agua Fria; near intersection of Daley Canyon Road and Highway 18. Has flush toilets. Open 5/15–10/15. Forest Service.

4. **North Shore Campground.** At northeast end of Lake Arrowhead and just north of dam; 0.5 mile off Highway 173 on Rouse Road. Has flush toilets. Open all year. Forest Service.

5. **Coldbrook Campground.** In city of Big Bear Lake, 0.4 mile off Highway 18 on Tulip Lane. Has some flush toilets. Open all year. Forest Service.

6. **Holloway's Marina and RV Park.** On Big Bear Lake, 0.5 mile off Highway 18 on Edgemoor Road. Has flush toilets, showers, laundry, groceries, snack bar. Open all year. Privately run.

7. **Grout Bay Campground.** On Big Bear Lake and Highway 38, 3 miles north of the intersection of Highway 18 and Highway 38. Has flush toilets. Open 4/1–11/30. Forest Service.

8. **Pine Knot Campground.** On outskirts of city of Big Bear Lake, 0.5 mile south of Highway 18 on Summit Blvd., then left onto Bristlecone Drive for 0.5 mile. Has flush toilets. Open 5/1–11/1. Forest Service.

# Big Bear Lake
# to
# Idyllwild

<u>93 miles</u> • Crossing the Big Valley

Although a large chunk of this section's riding is downhill, 93 miles is a long distance for mountain riding. An alternative is to camp overnight at the one of the campgrounds in the valley known as San Gorgonio Pass.

The route crosses the valley at a point where you will not encounter too much civilization or traffic. Then, after nearly a 4,000-foot climb, the section ends in the mountain resort of Idyllwild, a beautiful place for an overnight stop.

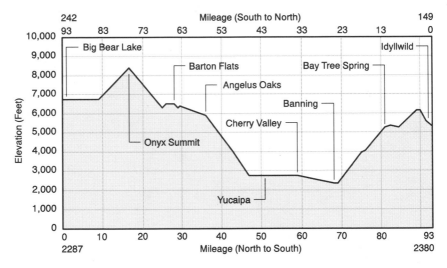

From the city of Big Bear Lake, proceed east on Highway 18 for 7 miles or about 1 mile past the east end of the lake to the location where Highway 18 makes a sharp left in Big Bear City. Do not turn left; instead leave Highway 18 and continue straight on Highway 38. Three miles later, as Highway 38 bends to the south, begin a 1,700-foot climb to 8,443-foot Onyx Summit. This is one of the higher points along the entire Trail; expect cool to cold temperatures. Vegetation in the area consists of brush and a few trees. From the summit there are 9 miles of downhill before beginning 5 miles of up-and-down work in the Barton Flats area (where there are several campgrounds). After 6 more miles of downhill is Angelus Oaks, which has a store.

Eleven miles past Angelus Oaks your coasting is over, and next to the Mill Creek Ranger Station turn left (south) onto Bryant Street. You will pass the

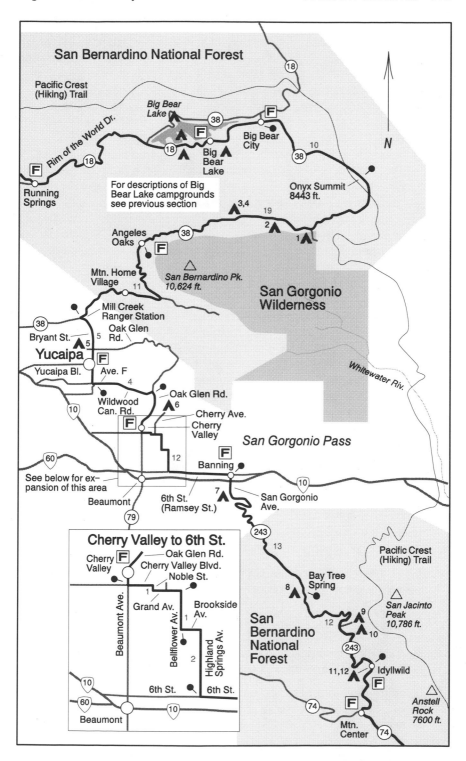

turnoff for Yucaipa Regional Park (#5) and enter the city of Yucaipa, which has stores and restaurants. While still in town and 5 miles from the beginning of Bryant Street, turn left onto Avenue F, which becomes Wildwood Canyon Road. Now heading east, bicycle gently uphill on this quiet, wooded, country road now being taken over by housing developments. Four miles from the start of Avenue F, turn right onto Oak Glen Road. Here grasslands predominate.

Oak Glen Road becomes Beaumont Avenue. Follow it into the town of Cherry Valley, which has stores and restaurants, then turn left onto Cherry Valley Blvd. After 0.5 mile, turn right onto Noble Street; after one block turn left on Grand Avenue; after another 0.5 mile turn right onto Bellflower Avenue. This farming area is being rapidly overrun with housing.

Ride about 1 mile on Bellflower Avenue before turning left onto Brookside Avenue; after 0.3 mile turn right onto Highland Springs Avenue; after 2 miles turn left onto 6th Street. Bike 4 miles east on 6th Street (which becomes Ramsey Street along a business strip) before turning right onto San Gorgonio Avenue in the city of Banning and passing over Freeway 10. Twenty-five miles remain to Idyllwild.

Continuing on San Gorgonio Avenue and after passing the Banning Travel Park (#7), begin bicycling up into the arid mountains. You will climb 3,900 feet over 20 miles. The road is in good condition and maintains a fairly even gradient. Gradually, the number of trees increases and the air cools. Thirteen miles from Banning is Bay Tree Spring — signed as drinkable in 1984 — and Bay Tree Flats Campground (#8). It is then 8 miles to the high point of this section at Pine Cove (6,165 feet). Three miles beyond is Idyllwild.

Idyllwild is a pleasant tourist town with plenty of stores. Its popularity can result in full campgrounds and motels during the tourist season although one can always try to share a camping site. The more one bicycle tours, it seems the less shy one becomes about approaching people for help.

## Campgrounds

1. **Heart Bar Campground.** Off Highway 38, 17 miles south of Big Bear Lake. Has drinking water. Open 5/1–11/30. Forest Service.

2. **South Fork Campground.** On Highway 38, 26 miles south of Big Bear Lake. Has drinking water. Open 5/1–9/30. Forest Service.

3. **San Gorgonio Campground.** On Highway 38, 28 miles south of Big Bear Lake. Has drinking water. Open 5/1–9/30. Forest Service.

4. **Barton Flats Campground.** On Highway 38, 29 miles south of Big Bear Lake. Has drinking water. Open 5/1–10/31. Forest Service.

5. **Yucaipa Regional Park.** 2 miles north of Yucaipa on Bryant Street, take Oak Glen Road to the west a short distance. Has flush toilets, showers, swimming. Open all year. County park.

6. **Bogart County Park.** On Cherry Avenue about 1 mile north of intersection of Grand Avenue and Cherry Avenue. Has flush toilets. Open all year. County park.

7. **Banning Travel Park.** On San Gorgonio Avenue just south of Banning and Freeway 10. Has laundromat, groceries, flush toilets, showers, swimming. Open all year. Privately run.

8. **Bay Tree Flats Campground.** On Highway 243, 14 miles south of Banning. Has spring water nearby.

9. **Marion Mountain and Fern Basin campgrounds.** Several miles off Highway 243 near Alandale Ranger Station, which is 5 miles north of Idyllwild. Both have drinking water. Marion Mountain is open 5/1–9/30; Fern Basin is open 5/1–11/30. Forest Service.

10. **Stone Creek Campground.** In Mt. San Jacinto State Park, several miles off Highway 243 near Alandale Ranger Station, which is 5 miles north of Idyllwild. Has drinking water. Open all year. State Park.

11. **Idyllwild Campground.** In Mt. San Jacinto State Park at Idyllwild. Has flush toilets, showers. Open all year. State Park.

12. **Idyllwild County Park.** 0.5 mile west of Idyllwild on County Park Road. Has flush toilets, showers. Open all year. Country Park.

# Idyllwild
# to
# Julian

80 miles • Dry, Pleasant Country

As you depart Idyllwild, the dense, beautiful forest is captivating. After Oak Grove, there is a 25-mile, 3,000-foot-high plateau ending at Santa Ysabel. Finally, the pretty resort town of Julian is reached. Temperatures can be high between Anza and Santa Ysabel.

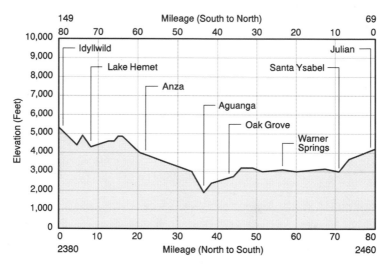

From Idyllwild, ride 3 miles south on Highway 243 to Highway 74 and Mountain Center. Mountain Center has stores and restaurants. Turn left onto Highway 74 and bike south a short distance to 4,917-foot Keen Camp Summit. Two miles beyond the summit is the store and campgrounds at Lake Hemet. From Lake Hemet, travel gently upward through Garner Valley on Highway 74.

In arid country 9 miles south of Lake Hemet, turn right onto Highway 371. There is a bar/restaurant at this intersection. A long downhill ensues. Six miles from the intersection of Highway 74 and Highway 371 is the town of Anza, with stores and restaurants. Fifteen miles from Anza on Highway 371 is the town of Aguanga with a store. This is a fine place to take a mid-day break.

At Aguanga, turn left onto Highway 79, head south, and begin a 1,300-foot climb through picturesque country. Six miles from Aguanga is Oak Grove (with no stores); 3 miles farther is a restaurant. After another three miles, at

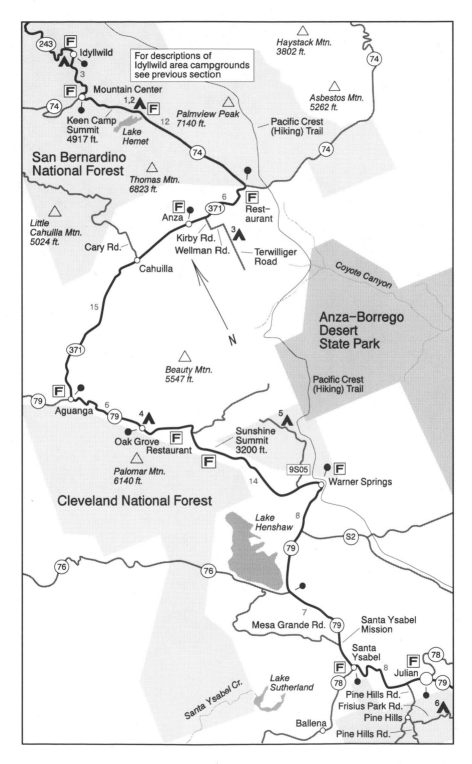

243 F Idyllwild
3
For descriptions of
Idyllwild area campgrounds
see previous section
F Mountain Center
1,2 F
74 Keen Camp
Summit
4917 ft.
Lake
Hemet
12 Palmview Peak
7140 ft.

Haystack Mtn.
3802 ft.
74

Asbestos Mtn.
5262 ft.
Pacific Crest
(Hiking) Trail
74
74

San Bernardino
National Forest
Thomas Mtn.
6823 ft.

F
Anza 371
6
F Rest-
aurant
Kirby Rd.
Wellman Rd.
3
Terwilliger
Road

Little
Cahuilla Mtn.
5024 ft.
Cary Rd.
Cahuilla

15

371

Coyote Canyon

Anza–Borrego
Desert
State Park

Beauty Mtn.
5547 ft.

N

Pacific Crest
(Hiking) Trail

79 F
Aguanga
6
79
4
Oak Grove F
Restaurant
Palomar Mtn.
6140 ft.

5
Sunshine
Summit
3200 ft.
F

9S05 F
Warner Springs

Cleveland National Forest

Lake
Henshaw
8
79

S2

76
76
14

7
Mesa Grande Rd. 79

Santa Ysabel
Mission
Santa
Ysabel
8 F 78
Julian
F 79
78
Pine Hills Rd.
Frisius Park Rd.
Pine Hills
6

Lake
Sutherland

Santa Ysabel Cr.

Ballena

Pine Hills Rd.

The Aguanga Market.

3,200-foot Sunshine Summit, there is a store, restaurant and motel. Beyond the summit there is a plateau that continues until Santa Ysabel.

Just before Warner Springs is a glider soaring center. This area is nearly treeless with some cactus here and there. Warner Springs itself, 8 miles from Sunshine Summit, is an expensive vacation home development with a gas station selling a few staples and snacks. The Pacific Crest (Hiking) Trail passes close by. On Highway 79 beyond Warner Springs, look for a solar electricity generating "farm" to the west.

After entering an area with more trees, 14 miles from Warner Springs, the Trail passes historic Santa Ysabel Mission. Stop in, visit, and get some cool water. A mile further down the road is the small town of Santa Ysabel with stores.

In Santa Ysabel turn left onto Highway 78/79 and begin an initially-steep 8-mile climb to Julian. The only campground near Julian is 4 miles south of town. To get there you must leave Highway 78/79 about 1 mile before reaching downtown Julian. For directions see William Heise County Park

(#5) below. Like Idyllwild, Julian is a mountain resort with all the amenities. If this is your last evening on the Trail, live it up!

## Campgrounds

1. **Hurkey Creek Campground.** On Highway 74, 4 miles southeast of Mountain Center. Has flush toilets, showers, swimming. Open all year. County park.

2. **Lake Hemet Campground.** On Highway 74, 4 miles southeast of Mountain Center. Has flush toilets, showers. Open 1/1–11/30.

3. **Kamp-Anza Kampground.** About 2 miles east of Anza on Highway 371, ride 1 mile south on Kirby Road, turn left and ride 1 mile east on Wellman Road, then turn right and ride 2 miles south on Terwilliger Road. Has laundry, groceries, fishing. Open all year. Privately run.

4. **Oak Grove Campground.** On Highway 79, near town of Oak Grove. Has flush toilets. Open all year. Forest Service.

5. **Indian Flats Campground.** 1 mile west of Warner Springs on Highway 79, then 6 miles north on road 9S05. Has drinking water. Open all year. Forest Service.

6. **William Heise County Park.** From Highway 78/79 one mile west of downtown Julian, follow Pine Hills Road 2 miles south, then head east on Frisius Drive for 2 miles. If you are coming from the south, turn off Highway 79 one mile north of Lake Cuyamaca onto Frisius Park Road and bike 1 mile west to the park. Has flush toilets, showers. Open all year. Country park.

# Julian
# to
# Mexican Border

### 69 miles • Hello Ocean!

This final segment of the Trail is a piece of cake — assuming you are heading south. The Trail drops from nearly 5,000 feet near Lake Cuyamaca to near sea level at the Mexican border. You can cross into Tijuana to experience the different culture.

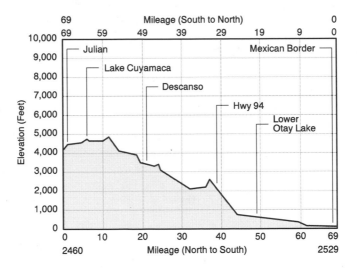

At the east end of Julian turn right onto Highway 79. You will have 1 mile of steep climbing, then a gentle climb of 5 more miles to the Lake Cuyamaca area. In this area there are trees and a store along the road. On the far end of the lake, Cuyamaca Rancho State Park begins. The park has some very pleasant, forested countryside, but Highway 79 can be narrow. The highest point of this section (4,870 feet) is reached 2 miles south of Lake Cuyamaca at Paso Picacho Campground (#1). Ahead of you is lots of downhill.

After leaving the state park, a good stopping point is Descanso General Store; this is the last store for 25 miles. To get to the store, watch for a junction in the road 9 miles from Paso Picacho Campground. At the junction, instead of following Highway 79 directly to Freeway 8, turn right onto Viejas Blvd. and bike 2 miles west to Descanso. After visiting the store, it is about the same distance back to Highway 79 using the more southerly Riverside Road.

From the intersection of Riverside Road and Highway 79, proceed south on Highway 79 and pass under Freeway 8. Continue as Highway 79 becomes

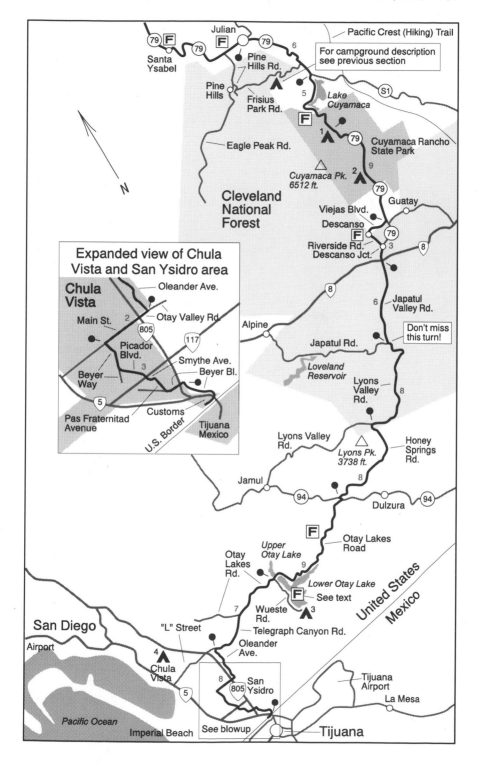

Expanded view of Chula Vista and San Ysidro area

Japatul Valley Road. You are now in Cleveland National Forest, although in this area the forest consists of brush. Heading south and downhill, there is an important turn you must make about 6 miles from Freeway 8. In a downhill stretch with a few houses and at a bend in the road, look for a sign which points toward "Barrett Honor Camp–3 miles." There is also a sign indicating Lyons Valley. Here, turn left onto Lyons Valley Road and continue south and downhill through lonely and oftentimes hot hills.

About 6 miles after the Lyons Valley turnoff begin climbing again. Two miles later turn left onto Honey Springs Road. Continue climbing near Lyons Peak for about 1 mile until you crest at 2,600 feet and begin a long downhill through Bratton Valley. Seven miles from the crest, turn left onto Highway 94 or Campo Road, then almost immediately turn right onto Otay Lakes Road. Ahead the route is fairly level.

Proceed down Jamul Valley. Two miles from Highway 94 is a Thousand Trails membership-only camping and RV park with a small grocery store which is open to the public. In this area, you may begin to notice the cooling and wind resistance of ocean breezes.

From the Thousand Trails park it is another 3 miles to the east end of Lower Otay Lake, a reservoir for the city of San Diego. At the lake's west end is the left turn onto Wueste Road for Otay Lake County Park (#3). The campground is 3 miles south with a small store at a marina along the way (open Wednesdays and weekends at last report). Some maps show Wueste Road continuing south past the county park, but a locked gate on private property prevents public access.

To continue on the Trail from the Wueste Road turnoff, bike about 4 miles further west on Otay Lakes Road until Otay Lakes Road makes a right turn. Continue straight on Telegraph Canyon Road for about 4 miles (entering residential areas of Chula Vista) before making a left turn onto Oleander Avenue.

Follow Oleander Avenue for 2 miles over small hills before making a right turn onto Otay Valley Road and passing under Freeway 805. Otay Valley Road then becomes Main Street. After 2 miles on Otay Valley Road/Main Street, turn left onto Third Street which quickly becomes Beyer Way. Travel about 0.6 mile on Third Street/Beyer Way before bearing to the left onto Picador Blvd., and after a mile on Picador Blvd. pass under Freeway 117. Picador Blvd. then becomes Smythe for a block. Bear right as Smythe becomes Pas Fraternidad Avenue.

After about 3 blocks on Pas Fraternidad turn left onto Beyer Blvd. and follow it as it crosses over Freeway 805. Just after crossing, turn right to stay on Beyer Blvd. and bike 1 mile, eventually crossing over the freeway again, to the border station.

All you need to spend a day in Tijuana is an American driver's license. Mexican officials may grumble about entering on a bicycle instead of in a car, but stress that you want to spend some money. If you intend to tour down the Baja Peninsula, contact a Mexican consulate for more information. I have bicycled in Baja California and on the Mexican mainland, and never had a problem other than getting safe water.

### Campgrounds

1. **Paso Picacho Campground.** In Cuyamaca Rancho State Park on Highway 79, 11 miles south of Julian. Has flush toilets, showers. Open all year. State Park.

2. **Green Valley Campground.** In Cuyamaca Rancho State Park on Highway 79, 5 miles south of campground #1. Has flush toilets, showers. Open all year. State Park.

3. **Otay Lake County Park.** On Wueste Road, 3 miles south of Otay Lakes Road. Has flush toilets, showers. Open all year. County Park.

4. **San Diego Metropolitan KOA.** In Chula Vista. Continue into Chula Vista on Telegraph Canyon Road instead of turning onto Oleander Avenue. Telegraph Canyon Road becomes "L" Street. About 1 mile after crossing under Freeway 805 on "L" Street, turn right onto 2nd Street and ride 3 miles. The address is 111 North 2nd Avenue. Has flush toilets, showers, swimming, food, laundry. Open all year. Privately run.

The border station near Tijuana, Mexico.

A well-equipped North Carolina couple pauses at Elk Pass near Mount St. Helens in Washington.

# What to Take

The following bicycle, bicycle accessory, and what-to-take recommendations may be of help if you are just beginning to tour and camp out. Consider the list a starting point only, and add, subtract, and modify as necessary. As you tour, you will learn more about what you need.

I recommend at least a 15-speed bicycle with very low gearing (with the lowest "granny" gear down about 20 inches). Most touring bikes are not sold with this kind of gearing, although some mountain (or all-terrain) bikes are. Your dealer can modify an existing bike to this specification. Insure that your bike matches your height and body configuration.

The debate goes on about touring bikes versus mountain bikes. I am partial to the touring type because it takes less energy to propel. Because most of the Trail follows paved roads, for overall use I recommend a rugged touring bike with dropped handlebars (which make possible a variety of riding styles); 1 1/4 inch, medium-width tires with puncture resistant inner tubes; and sturdy racks (such as Blackburn) to support panniers (bike bags).

However, on the non-paved portions of the Pacific Crest Bicycle Trail, a mountain bike would be the better choice.

I am told that bike manufacturers are now producing hybrid bikes which are a cross between mountain and touring bikes — they would be worth taking a look at.

Don't forget to pay adequate attention to your bicycle seat. Only use a seat that you are used to and are confident you can live with for a long distance. There are many good brands on the market with padding or gels of various sorts. However, once broken in, even simple all-leather saddles with no cushioning work fine — I toured with a Brooks for years.

Here is a list of items to consider taking on a long tour:

Bike Accessories

- Speedometer/odometer (the electronic ones are fun)
- Lights (which can double as flashlights) and flasher (for the rear of the bike)
- Reflectors (front, rear, and side — red reflective tape can be used to augment traditional reflectors)
- Air pump
- Water bottles (I carry four)
- Panniers or bike bags (available for both front and rear)
- Racks to support the panniers

Bike Accessories (continued)

- A handlebar bag (good for quick access)
- Front and rear fenders (keeps tire spray off the rider)
- Lightweight lock
- Handlebar cushioning

Clothing

- Light, long-sleeved shirt
- Three T-shirts
- Cycling jersey
- Two pairs cycling shorts
- Bathing suit
- Three pairs cotton briefs or panties
- Three pairs socks
- Thermal underwear tops
- Warm riding tights
- Insulated gloves
- Insulated windbreaker with hood
- Rain gear
- Compressible hat
- Knit hat
- Sweat band
- Cycling shoes
- Shoe covers
- Sandals
- Sealable plastic bags for above items

Tools and Spare Parts

- Adjustable (crescent) wrench
- Allen wrenches (those required by your particular bike)
- Other wrenches as needed
- Pliers
- Phillips and regular screwdrivers
- Chain rivet extractor
- Crank puller
- Freewheel remover
- Third hand brake tool
- Air pressure gauge
- Two tire irons
- Foldable spare tire
- Spare inner tube
- Tire patch kit
- Spare ball bearings for wheels
- Spare brake pads

Tools and Spare Parts (continued)

- Spare brake and derailleur cables
- Spare spokes
- Spoke wrench
- Miscellaneous matching nuts, bolts, washers plus wire
- Toothbrush for cleaning
- Chain lubricant
- Bicycle grease
- Grease cloth

Camping and Cooking

- Aluminum cook kit including bowl, pan, and pot
- Cup
- Plastic spatula
- Can opener
- Sharp knife, fork and spoon
- Lightweight stove and fuel
- Matches (in waterproof container)
- Detergent
- Pot scrubber
- Cooking oil
- Salt and pepper
- Lightweight tent with floor and bug netting
- Sleeping bag
- Sleeping pad
- Extra rope
- Clothes pins
- Sealable plastic bags for above items

Hygiene

- Cotton swabs (Q-tips)
- Dental floss
- Toothpaste
- Toothbrush
- Comb
- Fingernail cutter
- Shaving gear
- Soap
- Shampoo
- Sanitary pads
- Toilet paper
- Towel
- Washcloth
- Small mirror

## Hygiene (continued)

- Water purification tablets, drops, or filter
- Insect repellent
- Skin moisturizer
- High-SPF sun cream or lotion
- Sun block for lips

## First Aid Kit

- Band-aids of various sizes
- Several large bandages
- Telfa pads
- Antiseptic first-aid cream
- Aspirin or other painkiller
- Snakebite kit
- Chigger medicine
- Hydrocortisone cream (for poison oak rash)
- Vitamin A and D ointment for irritated skin

## Miscellaneous

- Helmet (lightweight, well-ventilated, safety-tested)
- Vitamins
- Radio (good for weather reports)
- Camera equipment, film, and film mailers
- Spare batteries for radio, camera, and lights
- Spare bulbs
- Pens
- Notebook
- Maps
- Address/phone number book
- Books
- Wallet with emergency and medical insurance information
- Compass
- Sunglasses
- Thermometer
- Sewing kit
- Emergency freeze-dried food
- Dog repellent spray
- Duct tape
- Bug netting to fit over head
- Bungee cords
- Stuff bags for sleeping bag, tent, etc.
- Frisbee

Creative packing.

# Touring Safety

No one wants a tour to be cut short by an accident or injury that might have been avoided — practice defensive bicycling. Here are some important precautions I recommend taking:

- Wear a bicycling helmet. Use a lightweight, well-ventilated, light-colored model.

- Always ride as far to the right of the roadway as possible, in single file. The only exception is on those backcountry roads that have virtually no traffic. When sharing narrow, high-traffic roads with wide vehicles, be prepared to temporarily move off the road if necessary.

- Wear bright colors, such as yellows and oranges, to make yourself more visible. Also choose panniers, handlebar bags, and even helmets of these colors.

- Avoid riding at night. If you must ride at dusk or after, use strong lights on the front and rear of your bike. Have reflective materials on the front, rear, and sides of your bike.

- Carry a first aid kit. Suggested contents are listed in the "What to Take" section.

- Always make sure that your brakes are working properly, especially before long downhills. Remember that the performance of your brakes will decrease when you tour with added weight. Don't let your downhill speed become so excessive that you can't negotiate a corner or you "loose it" if a tire blows. Stop on long downhills to let your rims cool.

- Always carry more water than you think you will need, especially in remote backcountry areas. Carry extra food.

- Protect your skin with a high-SPF sun lotion or cream. Shade your skin with clothing. Use a sun block on your lips. Wear sunglasses; they also keep bugs out of your eyes.

- Spend time getting in shape before a tour. Save your knees by using a bike with very low gearing. Treat yourself to some easy days.

# Information
# and
# Reservations

## National Parks

Campground reservations for the National Parks along the Pacific Crest Bicycle Trail are available by calling MISTIX (800-365-2267) or at any MISTIX outlet. For additional park information call one of the following telephone numbers.

**North Cascades National Park:** For information contact the park superintendent at Sedro Wolley, WA 98284 (206-856-5700).

**Crater Lake National Park:** For information contact the park superintendent at Crater Lake, OR 97604 (503-594-2211).

**Lassen Volcanic National Park:** For information contact the park superintendent at Mineral, CA 96063 (916-595-4444).

**Yosemite National Park:** For information contact the park superintendent, Yosemite National Park, CA 95389 (209-372-0264). For lodging contact the Yosemite Park and Curry Company (209-252-4848).

**Sequoia and King Canyon National Parks:** For information contact the park superintendent, Three Rivers, CA 93271 (209-565-3341).

## State Parks

**Washington State Parks:** For information contact the State Parks and Recreation Commission, 7150 Cleanwater Lane, Olympia, WA 98504 (206-753-5755) or in the summer contact their information center (800-562-0990 in Washington).

**Oregon State Parks:** For information contact the Tourism Division, Economic Development Department, 595 Cottage NE, Salem, OR 97310 (800-233-3306 in Oregon or 800-547-7842 elsewhere). For campsite availability contact the State Park Campsite Information System (800-452-5687 in Oregon or 503-238-7488 elsewhere). Reservations can be made by sending your request directly to the campground desired (no telephone reservations).

**California State Parks:** For information contact the Department of Parks and Recreation, P.O. Box 942896, Sacramento, CA 94296-0001 (916-445-6477). For reservations call MISTIX (800-444-7275) or visit your nearest MISTIX outlet.

Cactus flowers near Warner Springs in Southern California.

# Other Resources

### Bikecentennial

Bikecentennial is a national cycling organization dedicated to long-distance bicycle touring. The organization sells maps of long-distance bike routes it has developed, including coast-to-coast routes, and organizes tours along some of those routes. It also sells a wide selection of bicycle-oriented books including route guides and maintenance manuals by other publishers. Bikecentennial's annual publication, *The Cyclists' Yellow Pages*, is a gold mine of touring resources and is available to members. Bikecentennial: P.O. Box 8308, Missoula, MT 59807 (phone: 406-721-1776).

### Maps

American Automobile Association (AAA) maps and camping guides are valuable for tour planning. In particular, the northern and southern California branches of AAA publish maps covering parts of the state. If you are a member, getting their maps and camping guides is a simple matter of walking into a district office or telephoning. If you are not a member, have a friend who is a member get them for you.

United States Geological Survey (USGS) topographic maps show terrain in great detail, although some are out of date with respect to roads and buildings. The USGS maintains map sales offices in:

Spokane, WA at West 920 Riverside Avenue

San Francisco, CA at 555 Battery Street

Menlo Park, CA at 345 Middlefield Road

Los Angeles, CA at 300 North Los Angeles Street

Denver, CO at 1961 Stout Street

To order maps by mail for the western states contact: Western Distribution Branch, USGS, P.O. Box 25286, Denver, CO 80225. You will also find USGS maps at your local map shop and mountaineering shop.

# About the Author

Bil Paul lives in San Mateo, California with his wife Lorraine and three children. Every summer he leaves his job as communications specialist with the Postal Service to tour portions of the Pacific Crest Bicycle Trail.

His two previous bicycle touring guides, *Crossing the USA the Short Way: Bicycling a Mississippi River Route* and *Bicycling California's Spine: Touring the Length of the Sierra Nevada*, are both out of print. He also edited and designed *Mailmen's Dog Stories*, and designed and photographed *The Tri-X Chronicles*.